MORE
Country Walks Near
WASHINGTON

by
Alan Fisher

RAMBLER BOOKS

Baltimore 1985

MORE COUNTRY WALKS NEAR WASHINGTON

By Alan Fisher
Maps and photographs by the author

Rambler Books
1430 Park Avenue
Baltimore, MD 21217

If you notice errors in the text or maps, please point them out in a letter to the publisher.

Printed in the United States of America.

FIRST EDITION

Excerpts from "Life on the C. & O. Canal: 1859," edited by Ella E. Clarke, *Maryland Historical Magazine,* June, 1960, reprinted by permission of the Maryland Historical Society.

ISBN 0-9614963-0-4

CONTENTS

**5   Manassas National Battlefield
First Manassas Trail**

*Walking or ski touring — 6 miles (9.7 kilometers).
A short circuit tours Henry Hill, scene of the
climax of the first battle of Manassas in July 1861.
A longer loop leads through rolling countryside to
the stone bridge at Bull Run and eventually returns
via the route of Union advance across Matthews
Hill.*

**6   Manassas National Battlefield
Second Manassas Trail**

*Walking or ski touring — 7 miles (11.3 kilometers)
including the spur trail to Battery Heights. A loop
through rolling farmland and forest where the
second battle of Manassas was fought in August
1862.*

**7   The Washington & Old Dominion Railroad
Regional Park**

*Walking, bicycling, or ski touring — up to 30
miles (48.3 kilometers) round trip. From Herndon
to Leesburg (or vice versa) along an old railroad
bed that now forms a hiker's highway through
open country. Other access points are described,
making possible a series of shorter trips.*

8   Dranesville District Park

*Walking — 3 miles (4.8 kilometers). Follow Scotts
Run downstream to a waterfall next to the
Potomac River, then continue along the heights
and bluffs of the Potomac Palisades. Return
through wooded ravines and upland.*

9   Great Falls Park, Virginia

Walking — 4 miles (6.4 kilometers). Our local

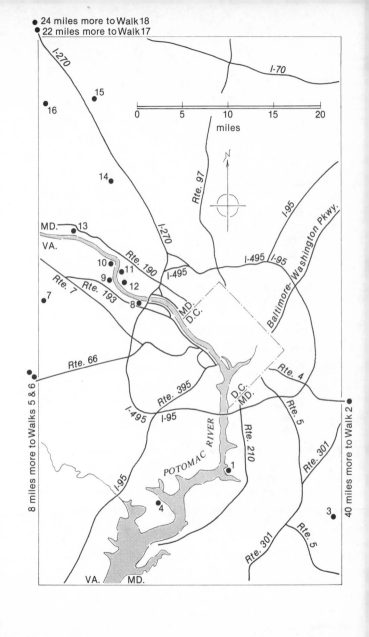

● 24 miles more to Walk 18
● 22 miles more to Walk 17

I-270

15
16

I-70

Rte. 97

N

I-95

14

MD.
VA.
13

Rte. 190

I-270

I-495 I-95

10
11
9
12
8

Rte. 7
Rte. 193

I-495

MD.
D.C.

Baltimore-Washington Pkwy.

7

Rte. 66

Rte. 4

Rte. 395

D.C.
MD.

Rte. 5

8 miles more to Walks 5 & 6

I-495 I-95

Rte. 210

Rte. 301

40 miles more to Walk 2

POTOMAC RIVER

I-95

1

3

4

Rte. 301

Rte. 5

VA. MD.

0   5   10   15   20
miles

Niagara and Grand Canyon. From Great Falls,
follow the rim of Mather Gorge downstream, then
descend into the deep ravine of Difficult Run.
Return to Great Falls on an old carriage road.

10 Riverbend Park
Walking or ski touring — 5 miles (8 kilometers).
A footpath extends for several miles along the
Virginia shore of the Potomac River above Great
Falls. Other trails explore the bordering upland.

11 Great Falls Park, Maryland
Billy Goat Trail
Walking — 4 miles (6.4 kilometers). Reached via
a short walk along the C & O Canal towpath, the
aptly-named Billy Goat Trail crosses rugged
terrain along the rim of Mather Gorge. Return
past Widewater on the canal towpath.

12 Great Falls Park, Maryland
Gold Mine Tract
Walking or ski touring — 4.5 miles (7.2 kilo-
meters). Easy hiking along the C & O Canal
towpath and the Berma Road (a dirt and gravel
track closed to motor vehicles). Continue around
the loop on woodland trails.

13 Chesapeake & Ohio Canal
Walking, bicycling, or ski touring — up to 22
miles, one way (35.4 kilometers). Hike from
Violets Lock to Georgetown (or vice versa)
along the entire section of canal that still holds
water and retains the appearance of a working
canal. Several access points at intervals of five to
seven miles are described, making possible a
series of shorter trips.

14 Seneca Creek State Park
Walking — 4 miles (6.4 kilometers). Follow inter-connected trails along Great Seneca Creek, Long Draught Branch, and the shore of Clopper Lake.

15 Little Bennett Regional Park
Walking or ski touring — 5 miles (8 kilometers). From Hyattstown Mill follow a gravel road along the valley of Little Bennett Creek, at one point fording the stream. Return along a wooded ridge.

16 Sugarloaf Mountain
Walking — 5 miles (8 kilometers). This small mountain offers sweeping views over the Frederick Valley. From the summit continue on a loop that follows a ridge across lesser peaks to the north, then returns along the valley of Bear Branch.

17 Maryland Heights
Walking — 5 miles (8 kilometers). A mountain battlefield and citadel. Maryland Heights is the southern end of Elk Ridge, carved into cliffs by the confluence of the Shenandoah and Potomac Rivers. Passing Civil War earthworks, the trail zigzags up the mountainside to a stone fort at the crest of the ridge, then descends on an old military road to the towpath of the C & O Canal.

18 Antietam National Battlefield
Walking — 2 miles (3.2 kilometers). Tour the battlefield by automobile, then stop at the Burnside Bridge, where a short hiking trail leads downstream along Antietam Creek.

Bibliography

PREFACE

As ITS NAME INDICATES, *More Country Walks Near Washington* is a sequel to my earlier book, *Country Walks Near Washington,* which describes excursions that are within reach of the city by public transportation. The outings described in *More Country Walks* lie farther afield, but all are easily reached by car.

It is customary, in books such as this, to include a catalog of cautions about adequate footgear and clothing, poison ivy, slippery rocks, and the like. Such a list follows, but more generally, of course, what is needed is simply common sense. Thousands of people yearly walk the trails described here without injury, but there are always those who are hurt or even killed because they fail to take ordinary care or willfully take extraordinary risks. Along the Potomac Gorge and at Great Falls in particular, between five and ten people die each year from drowning or falling off the cliffs. So, do not go swimming or wading, which are prohibited at parks along the Potomac because of strong currents. At Great Falls and elsewhere, control your children closely. Stay back from the edges of cliffs, and bear in mind that terrain that may present only moderate difficulty when dry can be treacherous when wet or icy. Where the trails are rugged, be careful and do not attempt anything with which you are not comfortable. Where the routes described here ford streams, do not cross if the water is more than ankle deep, and where the routes follow roads, walk on the left shoulder to minimize the risk of being hit by a car approaching from behind. Allow adequate time: two miles per hour is a typical walking pace for rugged terrain. And remember that the Washington region is inhabited by copperhead snakes, which are poisonous, so be careful where you place your hands and feet, particularly in rocky areas. On a more mundane level, during spring and summer check your clothing and body for ticks after your walk. In sum, use good judgment and common sense to evaluate the risks that are present under the particular circumstances that you find, and do not undertake any risks to which you are not accustomed, or for which you are not prepared, or which you are not willing to accept.

I have received information or other help for this book from the following people: John J. Adams, President of the Georgetown Pike and Potomac River Association; Marian Agnew, President of the Center for Environmental Strategy, Inc.; Michael Dwyer and Mark Walston, Montgomery County Park Historians; Dennis Fry of the National Park Service, Harpers Ferry; Bob Hartlove, State Forest Supervisor for Cedarville and Doncaster State Forests; Donald A. McCormack, Executive Secretary/Treasurer of Stronghold, Inc. and Patricia N. Holland, also of Stronghold; and John M. Sanderson, Park Historian for the C & O Canal National Historical Park. I am particularly grateful to Jonathan Edwards, Jr. and John D. Glaser of the Maryland Geological Survey, who reviewed the chapters that include discussions of local geology. Very many thanks also to my aunt, Mrs. Charles Edwards Rhetts, of Washington, D.C.

Baltimore, Maryland   A.F.
May 1985

1

FORT WASHINGTON PARK

Walking—3 miles (4.8 kilometers). A massive masonry fort of the early nineteenth century dominates the Potomac River below Washington. After exploring the bastions, parapets, casemates, and living quarters of the old fort, follow a hiking trail along the wooded shore of Piscataway Creek and around the perimeter of the former military reservation. The route also passes concrete batteries (now abandoned) built at the end of the nineteenth century. Dogs must be leashed. The park is open daily 7:30 A.M. until sunset. The fort is open daily at 8:30 A.M.; it closes at 8 P.M. May through August, and at 5 P.M. September through April. A visitor center and museum that occupy the commandant's house are open daily June through Labor Day, and on weekends during the rest of the year. Managed by the National Park Service (301) 292-2112.

WRITTEN FROM MOUNT VERNON, September 26, 1798, to Benjamin Stoddert, Secretary of the Navy:

> With respect to security against the attacks of an Enemy, no place can have advantages superior to the Federal City and Alexandria. Should proper works be erected on Diggs' point, (which you well know) at the junction of the Potomac and Piscataqua creek, it would not be in the power of all the navies in Europe to pass that place, and be afterward in a situation to do mischief above; for every vessel, in passing up the River, must, from the course of the Channel (and the channel is so

narrow as to admit but one vessel . . . abreast) present her bows
to that point long before she comes within gun shot of it, and
continue in that direction under the point, from whence shot
may be thrown upon her deck allmost in a perpendicular
direction. Should she be so fortunate as to pass the works, she
must expose her stern to the fire from them, as far as shot can
reach. Thus exposed to be raked fore and aft, for such a distance,
without once being able to bring her broadside to bear upon the
fort, you can readily see how allmost impossible it will be for a
vessel to pass this place; provided it be properly fortified
and well supplied. And what makes it the more important, is,
that it cannot be attacked by land with any prospect of success;
for it has the River on one side, Piscataqua Creek on another
side (each nearly a mile wide) and the opposite Banks very low,
a deep Ravine (level with the Creek) on the third side from
whence the height is almost if not altogether inaccessible. And a
very narrow approach on the fourth side. In a word the works
might be insulated, and one range of Batteries over another
constructed sufficient for an hundred or more pieces of Cannon.

Such were George Washington's comments and recommenda-
tions concerning the location of a fort to guard the water approach
to the nation's new capital, where the Federal government was
scheduled to take up residence in 1800. It was not Washington's
first communication on the subject; since 1794 he had been urging
the Federal government to acquire and fortify Digges Point. He
was, of course, closely familiar with the site, since it lay within view
across the Potomac River from his estate at Mount Vernon.

Washington was also personally acquainted with the Digges
family. In his capacity as a substantial Potomac planter and man of
business, Washington often traded and visited at the Digges estate,
called Warburton, where the plantation house stood on the plateau
just northwest of the large, present-day parking lot. Like
Washington, the Diggeses engaged in tidewater commerce on a
large scale. A letter to Washington dated April 7, 1775, states:

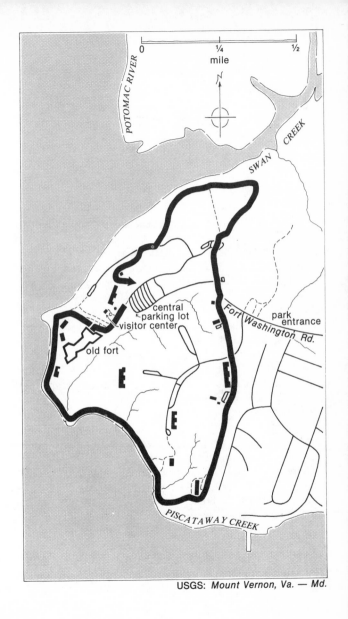

POTOMAC RIVER

SWAN CREEK

N

0 ¼ ½
mile

central
parking lot
visitor center

old fort

park
entrance

Fort Washington Rd.

PISCATAWAY CREEK

USGS: *Mount Vernon, Va. — Md.*

Dear Sir,

My Father & Mr. Hawkin's will take four hundred Bushel of
your Salt, & I will copy a few Advertisements to be put up in
this Neighborhood — your Vessel may come along side of our
Warf, which I apprehend wou'd be more Convenient for the
people that may want to purchase.

The family Join in Complts to all at Mt. Veron, with

Dear Sir

Your Most Ob Sert.

Geo Digges

Washington's diaries record frequent visits at Mount Vernon by
George Digges, whose nephew later inherited Warburton and was
one of the few people whom Martha Washington invited to her
husband's funeral. In his *Life of General Washington,* Washington
Irving describes the ostentation of the Potomac planters, some of
whom had English barges — or that is, large, sleek rowboats —
and Irving mentions specifically "Mr. Digges, who always received
Washington in his barge rowed by six Negroes, arrayed in a kind of
uniform of check shirts and black velvet caps."

During Washington's lifetime, nothing came of his proposal for
a fort at Digges Point, but in the first decade of the nineteenth
century, the need for a system of coastal defense became more
acute. Engaged in a protracted struggle with Napoleonic France,
England adopted a policy of seizing American vessels that were
trading with her enemy. British men-of-war also stopped American
merchantmen and warships in coastal waters to remove sailors
whom the British surmised to be deserters from their navy. In
response Congress in 1808 finally appropriated funds for construction of a number of forts to protect American seaports. For
the defense of the Potomac, the Federal government followed
George Washington's recommendation and purchased part of the
Digges estate, where a small earthwork mounting twenty-two guns
was erected near the water. According to General James Wilkinson,
who was one of the highest-ranking American officers of the day,
"This work was seated at the foot of a steep acclivity, from the

summit of which the garrison could have been driven out by musketry; but this height was protected by an octagonal block-house, built of brick, and of two stories altitude, which, being calculated against musketry only, could be knocked down by twelve-pounder . . . . "

Wilkinson was not alone in his low opinion of the fort. At the outbreak of the War of 1812, President Madison ordered an inspection by Major Pierre Charles L'Enfant, who had laid out the streets of Washington in 1791. L'Enfant reported that the works at Digges Point — by then called Fort Washington — were dilapidated and the guns poorly maintained. Concluding that "the whole original design was bad, and it is therefore impossible to make a perfect work of it by any alterations," he recommended the construction of a new fort, or at least the addition of heavy guns to the old one.

Fiasco followed. The War Department did nothing to strengthen the fort except to send a few men to the site to make repairs. Secretary of War John Armstrong argued that the rocks, shoals, and devious channel in the Potomac River would bar ascent by hostile ships, and that an invading army was unlikely to leave its ships at the mouth of the river and march inland forty miles. "The British would never be so mad as to make an attempt on Washington," Armstrong concluded, "and it is therefore totally unnecessary to make any preparations for its defense."

Armstrong's assertions were put to the test. In mid-August 1814, a British squadron appeared in Chesapeake Bay, and on August 24 the British army entered Washington, having marched overland from Benedict on the Patuxent River. Another British force sailed up the Potomac and captured Alexandria, meeting no resistance from Fort Washington, where the garrison fled after spiking the guns and setting a fuse to the magazine. The action was described by Captain Gordon, commander of the British squadron:

> The following morning, August 27, 1814, to our great joy the wind became fair, and we made all sail up the river, which now assumed a more pleasing aspect. At five o'clock in the afternoon,

Mount Vernon, the retreat of the illustrious Washington, opened
to our view, and showed us for the first time, since we entered
the Potomac, a gentleman's residence. Higher up the river on the
opposite side Fort Washington appeared to our anxious eyes,
and to our great satisfaction, it was considered assailable. A little
before sunset the squadron anchored just out of the gunshot; the
bomb vessels at once took up their positions to cover the frigates
in the projected attack at daylight next morning and began
throwing shells. The garrison, to our great surprise, retreated
from the fort; and a short time afterwards, Fort Washington was
blown up, which left the capital of America and the populous
town of Alexandria open to the squadron, without a loss of a
man. It was too late to ascertain whether this catastrophe was
occasioned by one of our shells, or whether it had been blown
up by the garrison; but the opinion was in favor of the latter.
Still we are at a loss to account for such an extraordinary step.
The position was good, and its capture would have cost us at
least fifty men and more, had it been properly defended; besides
an unfavorable wind and many other chances were in their
favor, and we could have only destroyed it had we succeeded in
the attempt.

After the British had burned the public buildings at Washington
and seized ships, supplies, and even stores of tobacco at Alexandria,
they returned to Chesapeake Bay. On September 8, Secretary of
State James Monroe (who was also Acting Secretary of War after
General Armstrong resigned in disgrace) ordered Major L'Enfant
to rebuild Fort Washington. For a few months work progressed on
a large V-shaped water battery, but by the middle of October,
when the British squadron left Chesapeake Bay and sailed for
Jamaica, considerations of economy reasserted themselves.
L'Enfant's intention to remove the old fort was questioned, and he
was told to account for funds spent and to submit detailed plans.
The tempermental French engineer took offense, and after refusing
to comply with the requests of the War Department, he eventually
was dismissed in September 1815. Lieutenant Colonel Walker K.

Armistead took over responsibility for the project, and work continued in accordance with plans that he submitted. Constructed at a cost of more than $426,000, the fort finally was finished in 1824.

Fort Washington was designed to defend against attack by wooden sailing ships armed with smoothbore cannons. The high, nearly vertical stone walls and brick parapets reflect the fact that smoothbore guns of the early nineteenth century were inaccurate and lacked penetrating power, especially at more than pointblank range. The fort's casemate chambers, where the defending cannons fired through small gunports in walls that were seven feet thick, could withstand a pounding even if the attackers managed to hit occasionally in the same spot. A mantle of masonry and earth over the casemate chambers provided protection against explosive bombs lobbed by mortars. The walls and ceilings of the casemates were far stronger than the hulls of warships, which were likely to be sunk or repelled before they could significantly damage the fort by prolonged bombardment. More guns were mounted in L'Enfant's V-shaped water battery, which lay below and outside the high masonry walls. (Much of the water battery was later destroyed to make room for concrete Battery White, but parts of the stone wall are still visible.)

Other, less essential features of the fort lack the Gibraltar-like character of the forward bastions. At the rear of the parade ground are the officers' quarters on the left and the soldier's barracks on the right. A guardroom and commandant's office flank the entrance archway. The commandant's house — now the visitor center — is located outside the fort on the hill opposite the entrance.

In the 1840s the fort was strengthened. The bastion at the south end of the soldiers' barracks was built to cover the approach through a deep ravine behind the fort, and gun platforms were constructed along the ramparts. Even so, by the time of the Civil War, Fort Washington's usefulness was greatly reduced by the development of large, rifled artillery and steam-powered, armored warships. Compared to the old smoothbores, the new guns had far greater range, accuracy, and penetrating power. Although rifled

guns were not at first mounted on ships (and suffered from diminished accuracy when they were), they still raised the spector that works like Fort Washington would be reduced quickly to rubble from a great distance by land-based siege cannons, as in fact occurred during the Civil War at several massive masonry forts protecting Southern seaports. At Fort Washington there was the additional likelihood that an armored ship could simply steam past the works at top speed, then shell Alexandria, Washington, and Georgetown at leisure. Accordingly, during the course of the Civil War, Fort Foote was built just below Alexandria, mounting a formidable array of giant rifles behind low, sloping, earth ramparts up to twenty feet thick. Fort Foote, however, was not completed until 1864, and until then Fort Washington was the capital's only defense against naval attack that never came.

In 1872 Fort Washington was abandoned, but in 1896 construction began on a group of new concrete gun emplacements around the old fort. The largest of the new batteries were armed with 10-inch disappearing rifles, which were lowered behind the revetments for loading and raised for firing. Until 1921 the new works, still called Fort Washington, were the headquarters of the Defenses of the Potomac. Other, similar batteries were located across the river at Fort Hunt. Eventually, these works in turn became obsolete, and in 1946 Fort Washington was turned over to the National Park Service.

AUTOMOBILE: From Exit 3A of the Capital Beltway in Maryland south of Washington, follow Route 210 (the Indian Head Highway) south about 4 miles to Fort Washington Road. Turn right onto Fort Washington Road and go 3.3 miles to the entrance to Fort Washington National Park. Continue into the park and past roads intersecting from right and left. Follow the main road to a large central parking lot near the old fort.

WALK: From the end of the large parking lot, follow an asphalt path toward old Fort Washington, passing concrete Battery Decatur, an observation tower, and the commandant's house—now a visitor center that features a short slide program on the fort. Enter the old fort through a large arched gateway.

After touring the fort, return to the bridge outside the main gate. With your back to the arched gateway, turn left. Follow a narrow path steeply downhill toward the Potomac River, passing to the right of concrete Battery White. About 75 yards inland from the point of land below the fort, turn left onto the River Trail, which is a wide hiking path. This trail provides easy walking at first, but it deteriorates toward the end; in wet weather it becomes muddy and slippery, so you may be forced to retrace your steps if the going becomes too difficult.

With the Potomac on the right, follow the River Trail along the water's edge. Continue as the path narrows and crosses small streams at the mouths of several ravines. Pass a trail intersecting from the left opposite a concrete trench. (This was an abutment where targets were mounted for rifle practice; firing was done from a point of land about 500 yards back along the water's edge.)

Follow the River Trail behind the target abutment and along the water's edge. Continue several hundred yards along the shore, then steeply uphill on a long flight of log steps set in earth next to a clay cliff. At the top of the slope, follow the path away from the water, through a grassy clearing, and to the right around a low, overgrown mound (actually an earth mantle in front of Battery Wilkins). Continue along an asphalt road behind houses on the right.

Emerge from the woods near a brick maintenance structure. Follow the road past a parking lot on the left. (Here and at other points where the route follows roads, walk on the grass along the left-hand shoulder to minimize the risk of being hit by a car approaching *from behind.) Pass to the right of Battery Meigs. At a T-intersection, continue straight across the grass and to the right of a brick building. Follow an asphalt drive to the right of another building. At a junction with the main park road, bear half-left, then continue straight across a road intersecting from the left. Follow the main road past the former parade ground on the left.*

Where the road curves sharply left, continue straight (thus crossing the road). Continue across the grass and then across a narrow drive next to a picnic area. Pass wooden posts and continue across the grass. Follow a gravel road leading half-right downhill between wooden posts. (The gravel road is to the right of a grassy swath that also leads downhill.)

Follow the gravel road downhill, then to the left. Continue past the water at Swan Creek, then gradually uphill. At a T-intersection with a paved road, turn right. With caution, follow the left shoulder of the road 140 yards, then veer half-left onto a wide, grassy path. Follow the path uphill past a brick command post on the left. Continue as the path curves left and emerges at the large, central parking lot.

2

CALVERT CLIFFS STATE PARK

Walking — 4 or more miles (6.4 or more kilometers).
Various trails lead to and from the beach and clay cliffs
overlooking Chesapeake Bay. Beachcombers can take the
most direct route; hikers can explore wooded ravines and
ridges. Dogs and swimming are prohibited. Open daily from
10 A.M. until sunset, May through Labor Day; open 10 A.M. to
6 P.M. (except Monday and Tuesday) during March, April,
September, and October; closed the remainder of the year.
Hunting is allowed in season in the area north of the service
road, so if you want to explore this area, you may prefer to
walk on Sunday, when hunting is prohibited. Managed by the
Maryland Forest, Park, and Wildlife Service (301) 888-1622
(Cedarville State Forest office).

S HARK TEETH. *Ancient* shark teeth. More precisely, shark teeth
from the early and middle Miocene Epoch — or that is, from about
twenty-four to twelve million years ago. The tangible remains of
prehistoric sharks are among the chief attractions of Calvert Cliffs
State Park. Just as tourists scour Florida beaches for seashells, so
fossil hunters comb the sand along the shore of Chesapeake Bay in
Calvert County, looking for pointed, enameled, triangular or Y-
shaped objects that range in length from half an inch to five inches
and in color from black through gray to white.

The earth cliffs along the Calvert County shore show a marked
stratification. The lower, fossil-bearing layers are made of fine
sand, silt, and clay deposited as sediment at the bottom of a shallow
sea that covered southern Maryland during the Miocene Epoch.
Algae and aquatic plants flourished in the sunlit shallows, which

formed a rich nursery for marine life. The climate is thought to have been like that of North and South Carolina today, and fossils show that the coastal waters teemed with varieties of coral, snails, clams, oysters, scallops, bony fishes, and other vertebrates, including turtles, crocodiles, seacows, porpoises, whales, rays, and sharks.

The fossil remnants of these animals are simply their hard parts — mollusk shells, vertebrate skeletons, and teeth — that did not deteriorate after the creatures died and their bodies settled to the bottom. These remains were covered and preserved by sediments that were carried to the sea by rivers or eroded from the shore by wave action. In the case of the Miocene sharks, only the teeth and larger vertebrae remain today, as shark skeletons are cartilagenous rather than bony and ordinarily disintegrate with the rest of the body. The thick strata of sand, silt, and clay in which the various fossils are buried now stand, in part, above sea level because of shifts in the earth's crust and also because far more water presently is amassed in the polar ice caps than was the case during the relatively warm Miocene Epoch.

The abundance of shark teeth found along the shore of Calvert County reflects the presence of great numbers of sharks, apparently attracted by young whales that made easy prey. A pamphlet prepared by Jeanne D. McClennan of the Maryland Geological Survey mentions that numerous bones of immature whales have been recovered in the area, suggesting that is was a calving ground. Many of these bones show the scratches and scars of shark teeth.

Another reason for the abundance of shark teeth is that sharks have a nearly unlimited supply. Arrayed in row after row, the teeth are anchored not in the jaw but merely in the gums. If a tooth is lost, as often happens, it is soon replaced by another that moves forward from the row behind. Also, young sharks replace their teeth frequently — every seven or eight days in one common present-day species.

It is likely that ancient sharks shared these characteristics, for sharks are among the most successful of nature's creatures, having remained essentially unmodified by evolution during periods that

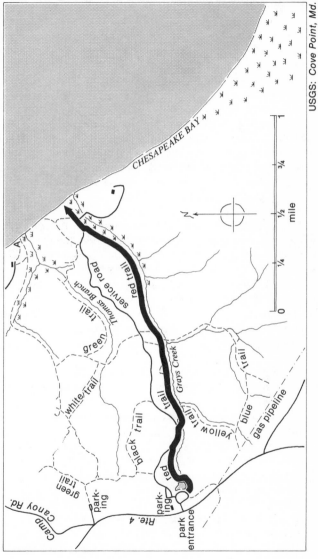

USGS: *Cove Point, Md.*

have seen the development and extinction of countless varieties of other animals. As old as the Miocene shark teeth are, they are of relatively recent origin compared to Paleocene and Eocene shark teeth found in places along the Potomac River; these two epochs lasted from sixty-six to thirty-seven million years ago. Even older remains occur in beds of shale near Cleveland, Ohio. Consisting of calcified cartilage and actual impressions of skin and body shape, the Ohio fossils are from a species of shark not very different from those alive today, but dating from more than 350 million years ago, well before the age of the dinosaurs. The fossilized remains of one of these primitive sharks can be seen at the Natural History Museum in Washington.

A final note. If you are bent on finding fossil shark teeth at Calvert Cliffs, the best time of year to look is early spring, after winter storms have exposed a fresh crop to view and before the area is picked over by summer visitors. The fossils are found at the surf line along the beach. If you do not want to get your feet wet, do your fossil hunting at low tide. At high tide, the water laps against the base of the cliffs in many places, so if you walk along the shore, be sure to return before the tide comes up. Do not climb on the cliffs or dig into them; after all, the cliffs are only clay and are prone to slumping.

AUTOMOBILE: From Exit 11 A of the Capital Beltway southeast of Washington, take Route 4 (Pennsylvania Avenue) toward Upper Marlboro and southern Maryland. Follow Route 4 about 45 miles to the entrance to Calvert Cliffs State Park on the left. If the gate is closed, there is another entrance about 0.5 mile to the north at the intersection with Camp Canoy Road, where a dirt road leads to a small parking lot for the Managed Hunting Area (see the map).

WALK: From the loop road at the main entrance, follow the red-blazed Cliff Trail to the right of a pond, then to the left across an earth dam and into the woods. Merge with the service road and follow it right 110 yards, then veer right along a brook to continue on the red-blazed foot trail. Continue more or less straight past trails intersecting from right and left. After following the edge of swampy woods on the right for more than half a mile, again merge with the service road and follow it right 100 yards. Continue straight to the beach (i.e., do not follow the road where it turns right across the swamp).

As the map indicates, there are a number of ways to return to the parking area. The service road is easy and direct; the green-blazed trail is more circuitous and scenic, but in places is not well maintained. If you are able to follow the beach north at low tide, a particularly pleasant trail starts at the water's edge just north of a swamp at point A on the map and returns to the parking area, as shown.

3

CEDARVILLE STATE FOREST

Walking or ski touring — 6 miles (9.7 kilometers). A network of trails and dirt roads explores more than 3,500 acres of woods. Dogs are prohibited. Open daily 8 A.M. until sunset most of the year; during winter, however, the state forest is open 10 A.M. until sunset. Closed Thanksgiving and December 25 through 31. The route passes through some areas where hunting is allowed in season, so you may prefer to walk on Sunday, when hunting is prohibited. Managed by the Maryland Forest, Park, and Wildlife Service (301) 888-1622. Telephone for information about camping and hunting.

YOU MAY HAVE HEARD of cruises to nowhere: a voyage without destination or ports of call, purely for the pleasure of being out on the open ocean. Here is the sylvan equivalent: a woodland walk to nowhere. This excursion follows footpaths and dirt roads through an extensive forest, without particular highlights along the way, but thoroughly pleasant nonetheless.

As part of the Coastal Plain physiographic province, Cedarville State Forest is flat but not altogether without topographic variety. To some extent the level terrain, which stands at an elevation of about two hundred feet in the vicinity of Cedarville, has been dissected by the headwaters of Wicomico River, an arm of the Potomac estuary. The streams have low volumes, low gradients, and correspondingly low erosive power, resulting in a branching system of shallow ravines. Zekiah Swamp Run, the Wicomico's main tributary, crosses Forest Road within the state property at an elevation of about 150 feet; thus, its average gradient for the

seventeen miles downstream to tidewater is about seventeen hundredths of 1 percent, or that is, less than nine feet of descent per mile. The swamp itself starts about a mile below the southern boundary of the state forest and extends uninterrupted to saltwater in a belt about half a mile wide.

According to a geologic map of Maryland prepared in 1968 by the Maryland Geological Survey, the Cedarville area — indeed, much of southern Maryland — is a vast sand and gravel flat. These materials are thought to be fluvial deposits and remnants of deltas left by ancient streams, including ancestors of the Potomac, Patuxent, and Susquehanna Rivers, that meandered across the plain in ever-shifting courses between five million and two million years ago. More recently, during periods of low sea level caused by the amassment of water in continental glaciers, these rivers entrenched themselves in their present courses, which are now partly flooded by a resurgence of the sea. The widespread deposits of sand and gravel may also be associated with former shorelines when the ocean, which inundated southern Maryland between twenty-four and five million years ago, slowly receded across the region. The picture is further complicated by relatively recent intervals of high sea level between periods of continental glaciation, but it is thought that the ocean rose no more than a hundred feet above its present level during these episodes. Finally, some sand formations appear to be remnants of ancient wind-blown dunes. In any case, covered by a veneer of meager topsoil, the sand and gravel near Cedarville are sufficiently free of silt and clay to be mined commercially, as currently is done in an immense strip operation immediately east of the state forest and at other nearby areas. On the state land, small borrow pits are visible where sand and gravel were dug for the forest roads.

The state's acquisition of land to demonstrate forestry techniques began at Cedarville in 1930, after a long period of agricultural decline and farm abandonment in southern Maryland. The name "Cedarville" is taken from a nearby post office, but the incongruous fact remains that cedars are untypical of the immediate area. Atlantic white-cedar usually grows in coastal freshwater swamps

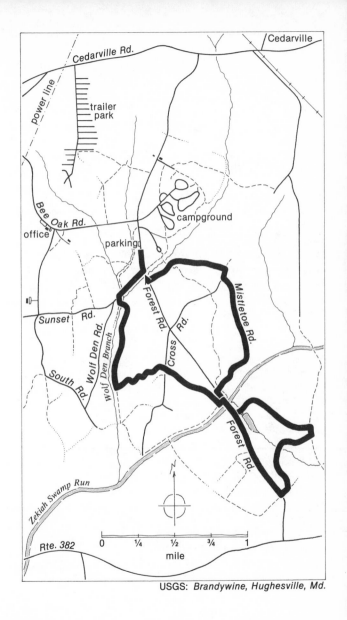

Cedarville

Cedarville Rd.

power line

trailer park

Bee Oak Rd.

office

parking

campground

Sunset Rd.

Wolf Den Rd.

Wolf Den Branch

Forest Rd.

Cross Rd.

Mistletoe Rd.

South Rd.

Forest Rd.

Zekiah Swamp Run

Rte. 382

N

0   ¼   ½   ¾   1
mile

USGS: *Brandywine, Hughesville, Md.*

or bogs, and Eastern redcedar (actually a juniper but commonly called a "cedar") is a short-lived species frequently found in overgrown fields. Redcedars may once have been common during the shift from farms to forest, but if so, they have long since been overshadowed by the dominant hardwoods and by stands of Virginia and loblolly pine. A vegetation map of Maryland prepared in 1976 by the Department of Geography and Environmental Engineering at Johns Hopkins University indicates that the upland within the state forest is dominated by chestnut oak, post oak, and blackjack oak — all species that are tolerant of dry, impoverished, gravelly soil. In ravines red maple, tulip poplar, river birch, and sycamore are common. Throughout the forest other common trees in decreasing order of frequency are black gum, white oak, sassafras, American holly, Virginia pine, black oak, beech, flowering dogwood, sweet gum, and various other species of oak and also hickory. This ranking, of course, is a generalization that may not accurately reflect conditions at any specific spot. And toward the southern edge of the state land, the dominant species are said to be willow oak and loblolly pine.

As a state forest, Cedarville is half park, half business. The area is managed for recreation (including hunting) and the production of timber and other natural resources. For the most part, the cutting of timber is confined to plantations of Virginia pine and loblolly pine, sold as pulpwood to papermills as far away as Pennsylvania and West Virginia. This walk passes a few areas that have been cut or thinned at different times in the recent past and that now show various stages of forest resurgence. Some tracts have been cut clear and left to themselves. Because many deciduous species (but not pines) can sprout back from stumps, this technique favors resurgence by hardwoods, which often are seen to have two or three trunks that once were shoots growing from a single stump. Other areas have been replanted with seedlings of loblolly pine, favored as a pulpwood because it grows faster and is more resistant to disease and to windstorms than is Virginia pine. When stands of loblolly pine are harvested, as occurred in the early 1980s in a large tract at the southern tip of the state forest, a common practice is to leave a few mature trees — about ten per acre — to repropagate the area; after a few years, when the seedlings are established, the seed trees are cut also. Another harvesting technique is reflected in aerial photographs taken in 1963, showing parallel swaths cut through stands of pine. These areas have been reseeded by the trees left in the adjacent strips, which will be harvested in turn. It is possible that in the future some of these timber operations will occur along the route described below, altering its appearance for short stretches, but the location of the trails and roads should remain unchanged.

AUTOMOBILE: From Exit 7A of the Capital Beltway southeast of Washington, take Route 5 (Branch Avenue) south toward Waldorf. Follow Route 5 more than 11 miles to a crossroads where McKendree Road intersects from the right and Cedarville Road from the left. Turn left onto Cedarville Road and go 2.3 miles to the entrance to Cedarville State Forest at Bee Oak Road. Turn right onto Bee Oak Road, then cross Dent Road and enter through the park gate. After passing the park office, continue straight on Bee Oak Road 0.6 mile, then turn right at a crossroads. Follow a gravel road (Forest Road) 0.2 mile to a parking area on the right, just beyond a concrete-block charcoal kiln. Occasionally, Forest Road is closed to automobiles, in which case you may have to park near the crossroads and walk to the charcoal kiln.

WALK: From the parking lot by the charcoal kiln, follow Forest Road downhill about 140 yards, then turn right onto Sunset Road. (Here and on other occasions where the route follows roads that are open to automobiles, walk on the far left facing the oncoming traffic in order to minimize the risk of being struck from behind.) After crossing a small bridge over Wolf Den Branch, go 25 yards, then turn left onto a footpath

marked with blue and white blazes. Go 60 yards, then bear left on the blue-blazed trail across a footbridge. Follow the blue-blazed trail through the woods, then to the right along a broad, shallow ravine. (The trail is also marked with occasional white blazes.) Continue along the side of the ravine as the slope gets steeper. At a low, wet area, cross a tiny stream, go 25 yards, then turn left on the blue-blazed trail where the white-blazed trail continues straight. Follow the blue-blazed trail as it zigzags through the woods, crosses a dirt road, and continues through the woods past several archery ranges. Eventually, turn left at a T-intersection in front of Zekiah Swamp Run and follow the stream bank 60 yards to Forest Road.

Turn right onto Forest Road and follow it straight past a road leading left to a parking lot. Follow the road as it gradually climbs past Cedarville Pond, located downhill to the left. Continue straight past an area where the trees on the right were cut in 1983 and '84. Eventually, turn left at a gate at the edge of the state forest, within sight of some houses. Follow a woods road 125 yards, then bear left. Continue as the trail winds through the woods. Cross a stream and continue through scrubby woods as the path deteriorates and becomes overgrown at points with saplings. Turn left at a T-intersection; in 175 yards, turn left again. Follow the trail through the woods and downhill below an earth dam at Cedarville Pond. Pass through the parking lot, then turn right onto Forest Road.

Follow Forest Road 300 yards, then turn right onto Mistletoe Road. Continue as the road becomes less worn. Eventually, at an intersection where the main road turns very sharply left (i.e., about 120 degrees left), bear right. Go 50 yards, then turn left onto a woods road. Follow the road to a T-intersection with Forest Road. Turn right and follow Forest Road to the starting point by the charcoal kiln.

4

GUNSTON HALL

Walking — 1.5 miles (2.4 kilometers). The eighteenth-century plantation house, outbuildings, gardens, and grounds of George Mason IV, father of the Bill of Rights. The house has been meticulously restored and handsomely furnished. From the boxwood terrace overlooking the Potomac River, a trail leads about three-quarters of a mile through the woods to the water's edge. Dogs must be leashed and left outside the buildings. A moderate admission fee is charged. Open daily, except Christmas, 9:30 A.M. to 5 P.M. Managed by The National Society of The Colonial Dames of America (703) 550-9220.

I HAD MANY occasional and strenuous coadjutors in debate, and one most steadfast, able and zealous . . . This was George Mason, a man of the first order of wisdom among those who acted on the theatre of the Revolution, of expansive mind, profound judgment, cogent in argument, learned in the lore of our former constitution, and earnest for the republican change on democratic principles. His elocution was neither flowing nor smooth, but his language was strong, his manner most impressive, and strengthened by a dash of biting cynicism when provocation made it seasonable.

So wrote Thomas Jefferson in his *Autobiography,* describing George Mason IV, a wealthy planter and Potomac merchant. In his triple capacity as trustee of Alexandria, justice of the Fairfax County Court, and vestryman of Truro parish, Mason exercised

great influence in local affairs. For three years beginning in 1758, he represented Fairfax County in the House of Burgesses, Virginia's colonial legislature. Although not a lawyer, he made a specialty of the exacting labor of drafting bills, resolutions, and plans for practical action. When the British Parliament imposed taxes on the American colonies, Mason joined other prominent Virginians in resistance. In 1765 he contrived a scheme to circumvent, in part, the Stamp Act, which required commercial and legal documents, pamphlets, newspapers, and other publications to bear revenue stamps like those now found on liquor bottles. In 1768 he prepared a series of resolutions, adopted by the Burgesses, urging that British goods be boycotted until Parliament repealed the Townshend import duties. As conflict with England intensified, Mason drafted the Fairfax Resolves in 1774, developing the issue of taxation without representation and again calling for a boycott of British imports; the resolves were approved by a meeting in Fairfax County and later by the House of Burgesses, which had been dissolved by the royal governor but continued to meet nonetheless. As a delegate to Virginia's revolutionary legislature in 1775 and '76, Mason was the dominant figure on the committee that prepared the Virginia Declaration of Rights — a forerunner of the Federal Bill of Rights — and the Virginia Constitution. During the Revolutionary War, he represented Fairfax County in the state's House of Delegates, taking the place of George Washington, who had left to lead the Continental Army. In 1787 Mason was one of the most active speakers at the convention in Philadelphia to draft the Federal Constitution, which he opposed in its final version, chiefly because of the lack of a bill of rights, later inserted as amendments the year before his death in 1792.

Mason was born in 1725 on the plantation at Dogue's Neck (now called Mason Neck) where he later built Gunston Hall. When he was ten, his father drowned during a squall while crossing the Potomac River. At age twenty-one, Mason came into the property on Dogue's Neck, as well as other large plantations in Virginia and Maryland, representing the wealth accumulated by

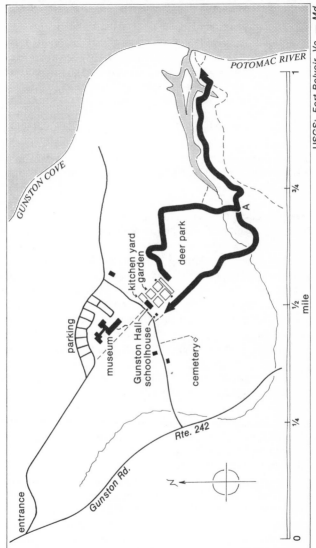

POTOMAC RIVER

GUNSTON COVE

A

deer park

kitchen yard
garden

parking

museum

Gunston Hall
schoolhouse

cemetery

Rte. 242

Gunston Rd.

entrance

N

USGS: Fort Belvoir, Va. — Md.

0   ¼   ½   ¾   1
          mile

his family over the period of a century. His great-grandfather, George Mason I, had emigrated from England in 1651 or '52, and had acquired land on the Potomac a few years later, when most of the area was still unsettled woods. Each succeeding generation of Masons had enlarged the family's holdings, and the fourth George Mason was no exception. To his five sons who survived to maturity, George Mason IV left fifteen thousand acres of Potomac farmland, most of which he had purchased himself. Each son received a plantation when he turned twenty-one, so that he could enjoy from youth the same life of independent means that the father had known.

In 1750 Mason married Ann Eilbeck of Mattawoman, Maryland, and five years later he began construction of Gunston Hall. He obtained the services of William Buckland, a carpenter-woodcarver who, at age twenty-one, had just completed his apprenticeship in England. Under articles of indenture to last four years, Mason paid Buckland's passage to America and put him in charge of completing his house. Buckland's compensation also included wages of £20 per year, plus room and board. He probably lived in the structure that later became the schoolhouse, where the Mason boys were instructed by a series of Scottish tutors. Mason was so pleased with Buckland's ornamental woodwork and elaborate carving that he recommended him to friends in Annapolis, where Buckland became an acknowledged master of his craft, receiving many important commissions.

Mason and his family finally moved into Gunston Hall in 1758. At that time, the Dogue's Neck plantation totaled more than five thousand acres, organized into four adjacent farms, each worked by groups of slaves under an overseer. The plantation's population numbered about five hundred people, mostly slaves. Aside from the usual farm buildings, there were several scattered villages of hewn log buildings for the hands and their families, as well as workshops for carpenters, coopers, blacksmiths, tanners, shoe-makers, spinners, weavers, and other artisans who served the needs of the plantation. A road from the house led downhill past an open park for a domesticated herd of deer and through the woods to

Mason's wharf, where tobacco and wheat were loaded onto scows for shipment along the river or transfer to ocean-going vessels. Mason managed the plantation without the aid of a steward and also attended to the insurance, shipment, and marketing of his crops. Much of the plantation's output was sent to England, so that during the Revolution Mason suffered heavy losses from the curtailment of trade — a small price, he said, to pay for liberty.

As a conspicuous member of Virginia's aristocracy of wealth, Mason was a friend and confidant of other nearby planters, including George Washington, who sometimes dined at Gunston Hall or received the Masons at Mount Vernon. On April 18, 1770, Washington noted in his diary that "Patsy Custis and Milly Posey went to Colo. Mason's to the Dancing School," an itinerant affair conducted in turn at the homes of different patrons. Typically, the children were brought from the surrounding plantations by their parents, who stayed to dinner and had dancing of their own after the lessons were over. At Gunston Hall dancing was done in the central hall, which during the summer also served as a family gathering place, cooled by breezes that swept through the door at each end.

Other rooms also served multiple functions. According to the recollections of John Mason, the seventh of nine Mason children, the left closet in the master bedchamber served as the upper pantry under the control of Mrs. Mason, who managed the household and directed the servants. The room most closely associated with Mason is his study, also used as a family dining room and even an informal parlor when Mason did not require to be by himself, as he often did. According to John Mason, "The small dining room was devoted to [my Father's] service when he used to write, and he absented himself as it were from his family sometimes for weeks together, and often until very late at night during the Revolutionary War." Even before the Revolution, "the family never were in his company but at meal times. He was always sent for when these were served and nobody sat down until he came in. He always had Grace said [or] performed that office himself . . . in the following words — 'God bless us, and what we are going to receive.'"

Describing his father's absorption in his work and books — for Mason read widely — John also wrote: "I have frequently known his mind, tho' always kind and affectionate to his children, so diverted from the objects around him that he would not for days together miss one of the family who may have been absent, and would sometimes at table inquire for one of my sisters who had perhaps been gone a week on a visit to some friend, of which he had known but forgotten." Of the garden which the study overlooks, John Mason said, "It was here that my Father in good weather would several times a day pass out of his study and walk for a considerable time wrapped in meditation, and return again to his desk, without seeing or speaking to any of the family. And in these walks we all well knew that he was not to be disturbed, [no] more than while sitting among his papers."

To the extent that public events and duties permitted, Mason lived a retiring life. From the age of thirty, ill-health became an increasingly obtrusive theme in his life. He suffered from gout, a painful and at times crippling affliction of the joints, especially in the feet, ankles, and knees. Mason also complained of a bad stomach. His chronic pain made him hypochondriacal and at times irritable. His wife's death in 1773 reinforced his crusty disposition, producing in him "a settled melancholy from which I never expect or desire to recover" — although he eventually did remarry.

In poor health, exasperated by the cliquishness and petty self-interest of many public officials, and bearing heavy responsibilities at home, Mason regularly turned down offices that were pressed on him — most notably an appointment as United States senator in 1790, when a vacancy occurred. For the most part, he confined his public service to his immediate community. Yet when he thought that his involvement could make a difference at the state or national level, he exerted himself without stint. Anticipating work on the committee to prepare an enumeration of rights and a state constitution, he wrote to Richard Henry Lee on May 16, 1776:

We are now going upon the most important of all subjects — government! The committee appointed to prepare a plan is,

according to custom, overcharged with useless members. You
know our Convention. I need not say that it is not mended by
the recent elections. We shall, in all probability, have a thousand
ridiculous and impracticable proposals, and of course a plan
formed of heterogeneous, jarring and unintelligible ingredients.
This can be prevented only by a few men of integrity and
abilities, whose country's interest lies next their hearts,
undertaking this business and defending it ably through every
stage of opposition.

Mason was as good as his word, drafting the Declaration of
Rights himself and managing to get it adopted with very few
changes of substance, "some of them," he said, "not for the better."
The state constitution was also substantially his work, although the
absence of a first draft in his handwriting prevents comparison
between his proposals and the plan finally adopted.

Following the Revolution, Mason retired from state politics. In
October 1782, he wrote to Edmund Randolph:

I quitted my seat in the House of Delegates, from a conviction
that I was no longer able to do any essential service. Some of the
public measures have been so contrary to my notions of policy
and of justice that I wished to be no further concerned with, or
answerable for them; and to spend the remnant of my life in
quiet and retirement. Yet with all her faults, my country will
ever have my warmest wishes and affections; and I would at any
time, most cheerfully sacrifice my own ease and domestic
enjoyment to the public good.

One subsequent occasion that he apparently felt demanded his
attention was the convention at Philadelphia in 1787 to prepare
the Federal Constitution. Making 136 major speeches, Mason was
among the five most active delegates. Mistrustful of the centraliza-
tion of power in the Federal government and unable to secure a bill
of rights, he refused to sign the final draft. He even issued a
pamphlet urging rejection of the Constitution by Virginia. In this

he opposed many of his life-long friends, including George Washington, who strongly supported the Federal plan.

When Mason died a few years later, his will summarized his attitude toward public affairs:

> I recommend it to my sons from my own experience in life, to prefer the happiness of independence and a private station to the troubles and vexation of public business, but if either their own inclinations or the necessity of the times should engage them in public affairs, I charge them on a father's blessing never to let the motives of private interest or ambition induce them to betray, nor the terrors of poverty and disgrace, or the fear of danger or of death, deter them from asserting the liberty of their country and endeavoring to transmit to their posterity those sacred rights to which themselves were born.

As for Gunston Hall, it remained in the Mason family until 1866. Most of the Masons who still resided in Virginia sided with the Confederacy, and their fortunes suffered accordingly. Nearly fifty years later, the Gunston property was acquired by Louis and Eleanor Hertle, who began restoration of the house and eventually gave it and 556 acres to the Commonwealth of Virginia, to be administered by The National Society of The Colonial Dames of America.

AUTOMOBILE: From the Capital Beltway southwest of Alexandria, follow I-95 south toward Richmond more than 6 miles to the exit for Route 642 for Lorton and Gunston Hall. From the bottom of the exit ramp, turn left onto Route 642 and go 0.9 mile to an intersection with Route 748 (Armistead Road) on the right. Turn right onto Route 748 and go 0.2 mile to a crossroads with Route 1 (Richmond Highway). Turn right onto Route 1 and go 0.8 mile to an intersection with Route 242 (Gunston Road) on the left. Turn left and follow Route 242 for 3.6 miles to the entrance road to Gunston

Hall on the left. Follow the entrance road to the parking lot.

WALK: After visiting the museum, the house, and the kitchen outbuildings, explore the boxwood garden behind Gunston Hall. From either of the gazebos at the outer corners of the garden, descend to a lower garden and from there to a grassy path running below the outer edge of the lower garden. With your back to the house, turn left and follow the path along the hillside, then sharply downhill to the right. Bear left at the foot of the slope and continue along the edge of a meadow (the deer park). At the rim of a wooded ravine, turn right. Cross a gully on a small bridge, then pass a trail intersecting from the left. Continue down and up across several small ravines.

At a skewed T-intersection (marked A on the map), turn sharply left. Follow the path as it winds along the top of a bluff overlooking a long, swampy stream and then a narrow cove on the left. Eventually, after crossing a bridge over an arm of the cove, climb a low bluff, then turn left at a T-intersection. Continue to the shore of the Potomac River.

To return to the house, retrace your steps to the intersection (point A) where the garden path by which you came turns right; instead, continue straight. Follow the path through the woods and gradually uphill to Gunston Hall. After emerging from the woods, continue more or less straight behind the schoolhouse, then turn left onto a gravel road. Turn left again at an avenue of redcedars leading to the Mason family cemetery. Return to the area of the main house to finish your tour.

MANASSAS NATIONAL BATTLEFIELD
First Manassas Trail

Walking or ski touring — 6 miles (9.7 kilometers). This large park not only commemorates two major battles of the Civil War, but also provides a rare opportunity to walk through an agricultural landscape of hay fields, hedgerows, rail fences, woodlots, and isolated farmhouses that preserve, more or less, the appearance of the mid-nineteenth century. A short circuit tours Henry Hill, scene of the climax of the first battle of Manassas in July 1861. A longer loop leads through rolling countryside to the stone bridge at Bull Run and eventually returns via the route of Union advance across Matthews Hill. Dogs must be leashed. The park is open daily from dawn until dusk. The visitor center is open daily, except Christmas, 8:30 A.M. to 5 P.M. (or later during summer). Managed by the National Park Service (703) 754-7107.

ON APRIL 15, 1861, six weeks after his inauguration and two days after the bombardment and surrender of Fort Sumter, President Lincoln issued a proclamation calling on the states that remained in the Union to contribute 75,000 militia to suppress the rebellion in the deep South. Four months earlier, South Carolina had seceded from the Union, followed in January and February by Georgia and the Gulf states. Exulting over the fall of Fort Sumter and outraged at the Federal summons for troops, Virginia, North Carolina, Tennessee, and Arkansas ultimately joined the Confederacy during April and May. At the beginning of June 1861, the

Southern capital was moved from Montgomery, Alabama to Richmond in order to cement the loyalty of Virginians and to place the Confederate government where it could respond quickly to the expected Union advance from Washington.

To the Northern populace, the location of the Southern capital only a hundred miles from Washington seemed a gesture of contempt for the Union's military capacity. According to John G. Nicolay, private secretary to President Lincoln, the North "saw rebellion enthroned in the capital of Virginia; it saw a numerous Union army gathered at Washington; the newspapers raised the cry of 'On to Richmond'; and the popular heart beat in quick and well-nigh unanimous response to the slogan." As time passed without conspicuous Federal action, there arose in the North a "morbid sensitiveness and a bitterness of impatience which seemed almost beyond endurance." Affected by this atmosphere, the Union army undertook what proved to be a grossly premature thrust southward.

The Union plan was developed by Brigadier General Irvin McDowell, the Federal commander in northeastern Virginia, where late in May the Union had seized and fortified positions at Alexandria and Arlington. McDowell proposed to attack thirty miles to his immediate front against Manassas. Located on the railroad connecting Alexandria and Richmond, the town was of strategic importance because of the junction there with the Manassas Gap Railroad, which ran west to the Shenandoah Valley. Defending Manassas was a Confederate force thought to number about 25,000 men. They were commanded by Brigadier General Pierre G. T. Beauregard, who had directed the siege and capture of Fort Sumter. In the Shenandoah Valley an additional 10,000 Confederates were led by Brigadier General Joseph E. Johnston. To discourage Johnston from reinforcing Beauregard, a Union force at Harpers Ferry was supposed to move south through the Shenandoah Valley at the same time that McDowell made his advance from Alexandria. Presented to President Lincoln, his military advisers, and the Cabinet on June 29, McDowell's plan was approved and the southward march set for July 9.

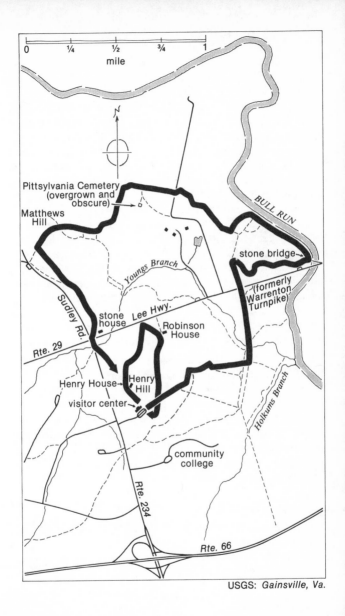

USGS: *Gainsville, Va.*

The plan was opposed by Lieutenant General Winfield Scott, U.S. commander during the Mexican War, and at the outbreak of the Civil War, the North's highest-ranking officer. Scott favored a much more methodical approach to the war and a much longer period of preparation before taking the offensive. He doubted the capacity of the state militia. Most militia field officers were unequal to their responsibilities, and the militia troops were unused to hard marching and lacked adequate equipment and training. In addition, the militia volunteers had enlisted for only ninety days, and their terms would begin to expire in July. Even the militia uniforms announced that the troops were amateurs: in many cases the men wore fancy-dress parade outfits, such as kilts or blazers and straw hats. Michigan regiments came to the war dressed as lumberjacks. Some Northern units wore gray. Scott proposed to send this motley militia army home. He wanted to assemble, train, and equip a Federal army enlisted for long terms, and then slowly strangle the South by blockade and by conquest of the Mississippi Valley. In broad outline, this is the course that ultimately was taken during 1862 and '63, after Scott's scheduled retirement was pushed forward slightly because of public dissatisfaction with his drawn-out war plan.

McDowell's column of 34,000 men began its march a week late on July 16. On the same day a Union force fought a skirmish near Charles Town in the Shenandoah Valley, but Johnston was not deterred from sending most of his men to Manassas, where it was known that the main Union attack would come. After all, for weeks McDowell's objective had been common knowledge in Washington, where the campaign was discussed with high expectations in the daily newspapers.

The railroad from Alexandria to Manassas had been wrecked by the Confederates, so the Union army had to march. As the head of the column began to move, the wagon train for supplies at the rear was still being organized. The advance was slow. "They stopped every moment to pick blackberries or get water," McDowell later wrote of his green troops:

[T]hey would not keep in the ranks, order as much as you pleased; when they came where water was fresh, they would pour the old water out of their canteens, and fill them with fresh water; they were not used to denying themselves much; they were not used to journeys on foot.

The first day's march was so exhausting that on the second day the column advanced only six miles. The troops paused to ransack the towns through which they passed, and some men burdened themselves with household items, tools, and even substantial pieces of furniture. Aware that their undisciplined troops could not cope with surprise, the commanders warily felt their way forward, with the result that the Union army required three days, and in some cases four, to reach Centreville, three miles northeast of the sluggish stream of Bull Run, behind which Beauregard had placed the Confederate army.

The Confederate line at Bull Run was eight miles long. Most of the troops were massed on the right for a contemplated flanking attack against the Federals. At the center were various fords on roads that ran south across the river from Centreville to Manassas. The Confederate left was posted at the stone bridge on the Warrenton Turnpike (modern-day Route 29, or the Lee Highway).

Like the Union army, the Southern troops were high on enthusiasm but short on training, experience, and discipline. They too wore a confusing variety of uniforms. Only the top officers were professional soldiers. General Johnston, who had arrived from the Shenandoah Valley, was in command because he was senior to Beauregard. Johnston had brought some of his men with him, including a brigade of Virginia troops under Brigadier General Thomas J. Jackson. The rest of Johnston's Shenandoah army, except for a fragment left to fool the Federals at Charles Town, was on its way to Manassas.

In response to the disposition of the Southern troops, McDowell decided to send the bulk of the Union army — 14,000 men — on a wide circle upstream, across Bull Run, and then down from the northwest behind the Confederates. While the Federal army assembled at Centreville on July 19 and 20, Union engineers scouted the river above the enemy's positions and eventually discovered an undefended ford on the Sudley Road three miles upstream from the end of the Confederate line at the stone bridge. To pin the Southerners where they were while the flanking move was in progress, McDowell directed other units to feign attack opposite the stone bridge and at the fords farther downstream. More than 10,000 Federal troops would remain as a reserve near Centreville, including some units that insisted on being sent to the rear because their ninety-day enlistments had expired.

The Union troops moved out for battle at 2 A.M. on July 21. One soldier said that in the dark the long column resembled "a bristling monster lifting himself by a slow, wavy motion." Again the march was delayed by confusion and at dawn the Federals were still north of Bull Run. Reaching the Sudley Road ford, the leading troops began to cross at 9 A.M., but the rear units did not cross until two hours later.

Meanwhile, the Union's diversionary attack at the stone bridge had begun with a slow, unconvincing cannonade. A Confederate captain of engineers, scouting to the north, saw the sunlight glinting off the muskets and artillery of the Federal column that was approaching the Sudley Road ford. He signaled to the Confederate commander at the stone bridge — a West Point graduate named Colonel Nathan "Shanks" Evans. Evans investigated and confirmed the report, passed on the news to headquarters, and without waiting for orders moved most of his force of 1,100 men to Matthews Hill, north of the intersection of the Warrenton Turnpike and Sudley Road. When the Union vanguard came into view on the Sudley Road, Evans's improvised line of defenders opened fire.

Despite their ponderous pace, the Union forces had achieved a large measure of surprise. Nearly half of the Federal army was coming in from the north on the weak Confederate left flank. But the attack itself, perhaps unavoidably, never rose above the character of the march that had brought the Northerners to Bull Run: the assault developed in a halting, jerking fashion that lacked cohesion and resolute impetus. The leading Union troops, consisting of four regiments led by Colonel Ambrose E. Burnside, moved slowly from a marching column to a fighting line two ranks deep. Then the men lay down and began shooting ineffectively. Only after two batteries from the regular U.S. Army arrived and began firing did the Confederates start to suffer significant casualties. Still, the Southerners repulsed two attacks by Burnside's men, who became so disorganized that they withdrew and took no further part in the fighting.

In response to an appeal from Evans, Confederate reinforcements led by Brigadier General Barnard Bee joined the defenders. To the north of the Henry House, a Confederate battery of four fieldpieces (positioned where a row of such guns can be seen today) began shelling the Federals from a distance. For nearly an hour — from about 11 A.M. until shortly before noon — the Confederates held the line north of the Warrenton Turnpike.

Gradually, however, McDowell pushed more Union troops to the front. He got word to the units facing the stone bridge to cross and join the attack. In response, a brigade led by Brigadier General William T. Sherman waded across Bull Run half a mile above the bridge. As Union pressure increased, the Confederates fell back, pausing for a brief stand behind the stone house at the crossroads. Then they ran southward across the Warrenton Turnpike, splashed across Youngs Branch, and scrambled up Henry Hill, where they formed a new line of defense reinforced by fresh troops. To the north the Federal forces, far superior in numbers, could be seen regrouping for a fresh attack.

By now the Confederate commanders realized that the main Union attack was developing in the vicinity of the Warrenton Turnpike. Abandoning the plan for a counterstroke toward Centreville from the fords downstream, Johnston started to order troops to move from the Confederate right to the left, then he abruptly rode off toward Henry Hill. Beauregard soon followed after ordering the redeployment of still more troops.

The battle was becoming a struggle for Henry Hill. Arriving shortly before Johnston and Beauregard, T.J. Jackson positioned his Confederate infantry and field artillery in a long line well back from the crest of the hill (as shown by the row of guns seen today east of the Henry House). From this position his batteries could rake the broad plateau that forms the top of the hill and his infantry could wait safely in the wooded hollow to their rear.

After a brief lull during the early afternoon, the long Federal battle line began to close in on Henry Hill. About 10,000 Union soldiers pressed the attack against about 6,000 Confederates, but at least half the defenders were disorganized and in retreat. Beauregard had arrived and was trying to rally the men who drifted to the rear; Johnston was farther back attempting to get more units up to the stopgap line. Shouting to his regiment, Colonel Francis S. Barstow told his two regiments, "General Beauregard says you must hold this position — Georgians, I appeal to you to hold on!" But immediately Barstow was killed, and the Confederate troops continued to give ground. Only Jackson's brigade at the southeastern edge of the plateau and Wade Hampton's South Carolinians in front of the Robinson House remained in formation. General Barnard Bee, whose field officers had all been hit and whose troops were in disarray, rode to Jackson and reported, "General, they are beating us back." Not visibly perturbed, Jackson is said to have replied, "Sir, we will give them the bayonet." Returning to a fragment of his men in the vicinity of the Robinson House, Bee pointed with his sword to Jackson's artillery. "Look," he shouted. "There is Jackson standing like a stone wall! Rally behind the Virginians!" Soon afterwards, Bee was knocked from his horse, mortally wounded, but at least some of his units reformed along the edge of the woods.

By 2 P.M. the open plateau at the top of Henry Hill had become a no man's land, although some Confederates still hid behind the Henry House. The Federals occupied the valley north of the hill, and the Confederates held the southern edge of the plateau and the woods behind, where many troops found time to reorganize. The Confederate right extended to Youngs Branch east of the Robinson House and the left reached almost to Sudley Road south of the Henry House. Describing the battle, John Nicolay wrote:

Reduced by losses, McDowell's numbers were now little, if any, superior to the enemy . . . a total of fourteen regiments, but several of which were already seriously demoralized; these were massed in sheltered situations in the valley along the turnpike and Young's Branch, mainly west of the intersection of the roads. All the advantages of position during the day had been with McDowell; now they were suddenly turned against him by the very success he had gained. The enemy was on the height, he at the foot of the hill. The enemy needed only to defend a stationary line; he must move forward under prepared fire. They were concealed in chosen positions; he must mount into open view. His men had been under arms since midnight — most of them had made a march of ten miles through the sweltering July heat. They were flushed with victory, but also lulled thereby into the false security of thinking their work accomplished, when in reality its sternest effort was merely about to begin.

There was another pause in the battle while Union batteries were brought to the northern crest of the hill opposite Jackson's guns. At a distance of three hundred to six hundred yards, an artillery duel began while the opposing infantry waited to the rear. Concealed in the woods and huddled behind the Henry House, Confederate snipers shot at the Union gunners. In response the Henry House was shelled by Federal artillery, and its mistress, Mrs. Judith Henry, an invalid of eighty-four years who could not flee, was killed in her bed. For a time McDowell himself occupied the Henry House, surveying the battle from the upper floor. South of the Henry House a Union battery was approached on one side by a regiment in blue. The Union officer held his fire, thinking the advancing troops were Northerners coming to support him, but the soldiers, who were in fact Confederates, leveled their guns and fired from close range. A Federal officer who observed the action from a distance wrote that "it seemed as though every man and horse of that battery just laid right down and died right off." The unmanned artillery became the object of a series of thrusts and counterattacks as each side tried to gain control of the guns.

Again and again Federal infantry advanced up the hill and across the plateau, only to be driven back by artillery, musket fire, and bayonet. As before, the Union effort was spasmodic; each assault was made by a separate regiment at a different point and different time. One Union brigade advanced southward around the Confederate right flank, but did not attack across Youngs Branch. Burnside's soldiers, who had seen action in the morning, remained well to the rear, and most of the Federal troops posted east of the stone bridge stayed there, despite orders from McDowell to join the battle. Perhaps worst of all, many Union regiments, having made a single charge and been repulsed, "went to pieces like the adjournment of a mass meeting," in the words of Nicolay.

By mid-afternoon the Union attack was losing momentum and the Confederates began to gain the upper hand. Reinforcements ordered north from the far end of the Confederate line finally began to reach the scene of fighting, and other units sent by train from the Shenandoah Valley appeared in unexpected places. Federal troops advancing west of Sudley Road against the Confederate left flank were decimated by fresh concentrations of Southerners. "Them Yankees are just marchin' up and bein' shot to hell," a Confederate officer told a friend who had just arrived at the front. Still farther to the west, a Confederate force appeared behind the Union flank and sent it running. At Henry Hill Beauregard led a counterattack that overran the Federal artillery. Suddenly Union morale collapsed and the Northern forces, without orders, began a general retreat. One Federal captain stated that "at four o'clock, on the 21st, there were more than twelve thousand volunteers on the battle-field of Bull Run who had entirely lost their regimental organization. They could not longer be handled as troops, for the officers and men were not together. Men and officers mingled together promiscuously . . . ."

Although disorganized, the retreat was not at first the rout that it later became. The Union forces simply started moving toward the rear, out of range of the enemy's guns. Most of the troops crossed Bull Run by the way they had come. A regiment of regular infantry from the U.S. Army served as rear guard, and reserves were brought forward to the stone bridge to prevent Confederate pursuit. In any case, the Southern army also was so exhausted and disorganized that orders for pursuit could not be carried out effectively. Confederate President Jefferson Davis, who arrived at Manassas toward the end of the afternoon, saw so many shattered units streaming to the rear that he thought the battle had been lost. There was also apprehension among the Confederate commanders that the Union army was planning another attack to the south with the forces that had remained at Centreville, and so troops were sent back to defend the lower fords.

Gradually, however, the Union retreat got out of hand, generating its own confusion and alarm. The traffic in supply wagons, guns, and caissons began to spill over onto the fields bordering the road. The mass of vehicles was swelled by the carriages of numerous civilian onlookers who had come out from Washington. The jam of troops and wagons became worse when the men who had retreated north to the Sudley Road ford finally rejoined the column on the Warrenton Turnpike. At Cub Run, a tributary of Bull Run, the road suddenly was blocked when a supply wagon crossing the narrow bridge was hit by Confederate artillery fire. Dismay and then panic gripped the civilians, teamsters, and soldiers who crowded the road and adjoining fields. Now and then shells, fired from distant guns, fell into the crowd. From the rear cries were heard that Confederate cavalry was coming, and people started to run. Soldiers dropped their muskets, packs, and canteens. Teamsters cut loose their horses, scrambled onto their backs, and galloped off. Although the bridge at Cub Run eventually was cleared, artillery, wagons, and even ambulances carrying the wounded to hospitals were left abandoned on the road, obstructing the progress of those drivers, such as photographer Mathew Brady, who remained with their vehicles. The formless retreat continued all night, during which one soldier told Brady that he was not going to stop until he reached New York.

McDowell telegraphed to Washington that he had been driven from the field and hoped to hold Centreville with his reserves until the retreating column could get behind the town, but a little later he had to report, "The larger part of the men are a confused mob, entirely demoralized. It was the opinion of all the commanders that no stand could be made this side of the Potomac."

In Washington the defeat created alarm that the capital itself might be attacked. During the course of the following day, the general awareness of defeat, disgrace, and possible disaster was reinforced by the dismaying appearance of the soldiers themselves, who shuffled into the city alone or in irregular squads for hour after hour, continuing into the night and the next day. Walt Whitman, who stood with other onlookers watching in silence, wrote that by noon on the 22nd, Washington was "all over motley with these defeated soldiers — queer-looking objects, strange eyes and faces, drench'd (the steady rain drizzles on all day) and fearfully worn, hungry, haggard, blister'd in the feet." Many of the lookers-on, Whitman said, were Southern sympathizers, grinning triumphantly, while other Washington residents set out food and drink for the broken troops, many of whom simply flopped down on the sidewalks and in vacant lots and fell asleep in the rain.

Steps were taken to secure the city. Each regiment was assigned a location where it could receive rations and reassemble. Fresh troops were rushed to Washington. There was, however, no effort by the Confederates to march on the Federal capital. General Johnston wrote to Jefferson Davis that his army was in disarray: "Everybody, officer & private, seemed to think that he had fulfilled all his obligations to country — & that before attending to any further call of duty, it was his privilege to look after his friends, procure trophies, or amuse himself. It was several days after you left us before the regiments who really fought could be reassembled." Johnston later enlarged on this theme:

The Confederate army was more disorganized by victory than that of the United States by defeat. The Southern volunteers believed that the objects of the war had been accomplished by their victory, and that they had achieved all that their country required of them. Many, therefore, in ignorance of their military obligations, left the army, not to return. Some hastened home to

exhibit the trophies picked up on the field; others left their
regiments without ceremony to attend to wounded friends,
frequently accompanying them to hospitals in distant towns.
Such were the reports of general and staff officers and railroad
officials. Exaggerated ideas of victory prevailing among our
troops cost us more men than the Federal army lost by defeat.

The actual casualties suffered by the two armies were not far out
of balance: 481 Federals killed and 1,011 wounded, compared to
387 Confederate dead and 1,582 wounded. The South also took
about 1,500 prisoners, many of them wounded. In concrete terms,
the Confederacy's chief gain from the victory was the immense
haul of Federal arms abandoned on the battlefield and route of
retreat. Beauregard reported capturing twenty-eight fieldpieces,
thirty-seven caissons, and huge quantities of muskets, ammunition,
blankets, haversacks, and hospital supplies. Also, mercantile firms
in Europe concluded that the Confederacy was here to stay and
that the self-proclaimed nation offered a credit-worthy opportunity
for the sale of essential goods, including munitions, previously
supplied to Southern states by the North.

As days and weeks passed, however, the battle quickly lost
whatever military significance it might have had. Except for
pickets posted toward Washington, the Confederates advanced no
farther than Fairfax Courthouse. At Washington the Union army
dug in, and during the following months it regained and surpassed
its earlier strength.

The illusion on both sides that the war would be a brief affair
began to dissipate. Even prior to the defeat at Bull Run, the Federal
government had begun to prepare for a protracted war of attrition
based on the Union's overwhelming advantage in naval strength,
manpower, war industry, and finance. Meeting in emergency
session at the beginning of July, Congress approved Lincoln's
executive directive for the formation of a Federal army of 500,000
men enlisted for three-year terms, a national expenditure of $250
million, and a strengthened navy to enforce a blockade of Southern

ports. For more than half a year after Bull Run the Virginia front was quiet, except for a few incidents, while the North again prepared to march on Richmond.

AUTOMOBILE: From Exit 9 of the Capital Beltway (I-495) west of Arlington, follow Route 66 west about 17 miles to Route 234 north for Manassas National Battlefield Park. Follow Route 234 for 0.7 mile to the entrance road for the visitor center on the right.

WALK: The walk described in subsequent paragraphs follows (for the most part) the First Manassas Trail; however, the mile-long Henry Hill Walking Tour, which provides an overview of the first battle of Manassas, is a good way to begin your excursion. The tour starts behind the visitor center and is marked by a series of signs and interpretive stations. The route proceeds past cannons to the Henry House, then to a point by Lee Highway (formerly the Warrenton Turnpike), before looping back past the Robinson House and more cannons located along the line of defense established by Stonewall Jackson. Return to the parking lot in front of the visitor center.

To continue for a walk of 5 miles on the First Manassas Trail, start from the parking lot in front of the visitor center. Facing the visitor center, turn right and follow a worn track across a level field about a hundred yards to the right (or rear) of an equestrian statue of General Jackson. After passing through a row of artillery, pick up the First Manassas Trail, which is marked by occasional blue blazes. (A sign indicates that the trail is 9.1 miles long; the walk described here, however, is only 5 miles long because it omits the last section of the First Manassas Trail.)

Follow the First Manassas Trail downhill through a row of redcedars, across a small meadow, and through a short stretch of woods. Pass a narrow, blue-blazed footpath that leads right. With forest on the right and a field on the left, follow the main trail along the edge of the woods, which bends first left, then right. Continue past a yellow-blazed horse trail intersecting from the right.

After passing through a gap in a hedgerow, bear right through another hedgerow. Two trails lead diagonally downhill across the field; follow the left-hand trail across a small stream and continue uphill. At a four-way trail intersection just beyond a row of redcedars, turn left onto a gravel road that leads downhill to Youngs Branch.

If the water level in Youngs Branch is low (as it usually is), ford the stream and continue straight on a dirt road past a trail leading right. Where the dirt road veers right at the top of the slope, continue straight on the blue-blazed footpath to Lee Highway. Cross the road with care and follow the blue-blazed trail uphill. At a knoll in front of a large field, turn very sharply right onto a path marked with a symbol resembling a white three-leafed clover. (This trail, which is also marked with blue blazes, forms a loop leading to the stone bridge.) Follow the white cloverleaves and blue blazes across another knoll, then to the left downhill. Continue along a boardwalk to a parking lot and from there downhill to the stone bridge, site of the left flank of the Confederate army at the outset of the first battle of Manassas. The Federal forces tried to outflank the Confederates by crossing upstream at the Sudley Road ford.

From the bridge, turn left upstream along Bull Run, keeping the creek on the right. Pass straight through a junction where the blue-blazed trail leads left; continue uphill along the water's edge and straight on the white cloverleaf trail through another junction at the top of a *steep bluff above Bull Run. Soon the cloverleaf trail veers left away from Bull Run and along the rim of a ravine.*

When the trail reaches a field, turn right along the edge of the woods (i.e., toward Pittsylvania Cemetery on the blue-blazed trail, according to a park sign). At a corner of the woods, bear half-right and continue across open meadow to another corner of the forest in the distance. Continue along the edge of the woods and eventually across a farm road.

Follow the blue-blazed trail into the woods. Continue for more than a mile, passing several paths intersecting from the left and, at one point, passing straight through a four-way intersection with the yellow-blazed horse path. Eventually, emerge from the woods and continue straight across a meadow to a row of guns.

From the artillery, advance across the meadow in the direction toward which the guns are pointed — i.e., toward the visitor center and the Henry House on Henry Hill in the distance. This is the route of the Union advance. If the grass is too high or too wet to be agreeable, a mown path runs parallel with Sudley Road farther to the right.

Continue across knolls and downhill past a stone house to the intersection of Lee Highway and Sudley Road. With care, cross Lee Highway and follow the shoulder of Sudley Road 75 yards across a bridge over Youngs Branch. Once across the bridge, veer half-left into the meadow and climb to the Henry House (there is no set path). From the Henry House, return to the visitor center.

6

MANASSAS NATIONAL BATTLEFIELD
Second Manassas Trail

*Walking or ski touring — 7 miles (11.3 kilometers) including
the spur trail to Battery Heights. A loop through rolling
farmland and forest where the second battle of Manassas was
fought in August 1862. In part the trail follows the unfinished
railroad where Stonewall Jackson's troops repeatedly
repulsed Union attacks. A spur trail leads to Battery Heights,
where the battle began. Continue through fields and woods
to Chinn Ridge, across which Union troops eventually
retreated. Dogs must be leashed. The park is open daily from
dawn until dusk. The visitor center is open daily, except
Christmas, 8:30 A.M. to 5 P.M. (or later during summer).
Managed by the National Park Service (703) 754-7107.*

LATE IN JUNE 1862, Major General John Pope, who had
fought well against the Confederates in the Mississippi Valley, was
brought east to command various Federal contingents that had
been floundering in northern Virginia. Pope's newly-organized
force of 50,000 men was termed the Army of Virginia, and in July
he set about concentrating his army at Sperryville, south of the
Rappahannock River and not far east of the Blue Ridge. The
Confederate army that had crushed the Union advance at
Manassas the year before had been pulled south for the defense of
Richmond. (For a discussion of the first battle of Manassas, see
Chapter 5.) Even Stonewall Jackson's force of 17,000 men —
which throughout the spring had bedeviled the Federals in the
Shenandoah Valley and had stymied Union advance from the

north — was withdrawn to Richmond late in June to help repel the attack from the east by the Union Army of the Potomac.

Led by Major General George B. McClellan, the Army of the Potomac had landed at Newport News late in March, and during April and May had advanced slowly west toward Richmond along the peninsula between the James and York Rivers. On May 31 the Confederate commander, General Joseph E. Johnston, had been severely wounded, and the next day General Robert E. Lee was placed at the head of the army that he was to lead for the rest of the war. During the last week of June, Lee attacked and repulsed the Federals near Richmond. After the Army of the Potomac drew back to a fortified camp on the James River, McClellan's peninsula campaign stagnated.

Lee now decided that the time had come to "suppress" (as he put it) Pope's growing army in northern Virginia. He wanted to smash the Yankees before Pope and McClellan joined forces, a combination that would total roughly 140,000 Federals against Lee's army of 70,000 or 80,000 men. Earlier Lee had pointedly renamed the troops under his command the Army of *Northern* Virginia, and in mid-July, when the Army of the Potomac was still only twenty-five miles from Richmond, Lee started moving detachments of his army north. On July 13 he sent Stonewall Jackson with 12,000 men to Gordonsville, a key railroad junction that was closer to Pope's army than to Richmond. Both Pope and McClellan learned of the move but did nothing. Encouraged by Federal inaction, Lee sent still more troops to join Jackson, who attacked Pope's forward units near Culpeper on August 9, forcing the Federals to retreat. The battle again disclosed to the Union leadership that a large part of Lee's army had left Richmond, but McClellan, who was in a position to strike, remained inert. Lee rightly judged that McClellan's campaign was moribund; in fact, on August 3 McClellan had been ordered to withdraw north, where his army could join Pope. By mid-August Lee had reduced the Confederate forces at Richmond to fewer than 25,000 men opposing 90,000 Federals. Then Lee himself left Richmond to take

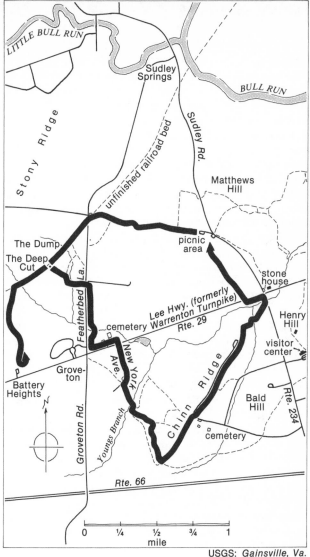

LITTLE BULL RUN

Sudley
Springs

BULL RUN

Stony Ridge

unfinished railroad bed

Sudley Rd.

Matthews
Hill

The Dump

The Deep
Cut

picnic
area

stone
house

Featherbed La.

Lee Hwy. (formerly
Warrenton Turnpike)
cemetery   Rte. 29

Henry
Hill

visitor
center

New York Ave.

Chinn Ridge

Groveton

Battery
Heights

N

Groveton Rd.

Youngs Branch

Bald
Hill

cemetery

Rte. 234

Rte. 66

0   ¼   ½   ¾   1
mile

USGS: *Gainsville, Va.*

charge of the large Confederate army, now about 55,000 strong, that was in the field. The suppression of John Pope was under way.

In numbers, if not in spirit or experience, Pope's army in mid-August equaled Lee's, and overwhelming Federal reinforcements were expected. Pope had received orders from Henry Halleck, general-in-chief of the U.S. Army, directing him to stay where he was until he was joined by 70,000 or more troops from McClellan's army. But McClellan was dragging his feet. He and many of his staff were stung by the order to abandon their position east of Richmond and to reinforce Pope, whom they regarded as an upstart; they thought Pope's army should join them. Major General Ambrose Burnside, who had a corps of men with Pope, called "treasonous" the talk that he heard during a visit to McClellan's camp. One of McClellan's officers wrote on August 11, "I have one hope left; when that ass Pope shall have lost his army, and when Washington shall again be menaced (say in six days from this time) then and only then will they find out that our little General is not in his right place and then they will call loudly for his aid." Not until August 14, eleven days after receiving orders to move north, did McClellan begin to send his troops toward a rendevous with Pope, whom he was glad to hear was in trouble. While still near Richmond, McClellan wrote to his wife on August 21: "I believe I have triumphed!! Just received a telegram from Halleck stating that Pope and Burnside are very hard pressed."

Pope was indeed hard pressed. By August 19 he had retreated north of the Rappahannock River, narrowly escaping a move by Lee to cut him off. Guarding the river crossings, Pope continued to wait for reinforcements, which were beginning to arrive. By August 22 he had 70,000 men, and more were on the way.

Unable to attack directly across the Rappahannock, Lee again divided his forces, despite the standard cautions of military theory. He sent 25,000 men under Stonewall Jackson on a long march to the northwest around Pope's position on the river. Lee would linger briefly to delude Pope that the Confederates were still to his south, then follow Jackson for an attack on Pope's rear.

Leaving at dawn on August 25, Jackson's "foot cavalry," as his hard-marching veterans were called, covered more than fifty miles in forty hours. They crossed the Rappahannock far upstream, then swung southeast to intercept the Orange & Alexandria Railroad — Pope's supply line — on the evening of August 26. The next day Jackson's troops moved northeast along the railroad to Manassas Junction, where they rested, gorged themselves on Federal food supplies, and burned warehouses crammed with Union stores. That night they marched off in several directions to confuse the Federals, then regrouped the next day, August 28, on a wooded ridge overlooking the Warrenton Turnpike, a mile or two northwest of the fields where the first battle of Manassas had been fought.

Jackson was causing serious trouble, but his position was precarious. He risked being caught between Federal reinforcements advancing from Alexandria and Pope's large army to the south. Jackson was supposed to be joined by Lee, who had moved northwest on August 26, but the following day Pope ordered his own army northward to keep Lee and Jackson apart. Pope directed various units to assemble in the vicinity of Gainsville, west of Manassas. Other detachments were told to converge on Manassas to smash Jackson, but by the time the Federals arrived, the Confederates were gone. Throughout the day on August 28, Union columns marched back and forth to Centreville and elsewhere, pursuing reports of Jackson's movements. Late in the afternoon, however, Jackson himself announced his position by attacking a division of 6,000 Federals marching east on the Warrenton Turnpike near the crossroads at Groveton (see the map).

The attack came shortly before sunset. A Confederate officer recalled "a hoarse roar like that from cages of wild beasts at the scent of blood" as the Southerners, who had been concealed in the woods on Stony Ridge, fell into ranks. Confederate artillery rolled into the open, unlimbered, and began firing. The infantry paraded out of the trees and down the gentle slope toward the turnpike, swung into line next to the fieldpieces, and started shooting. The

Federal column on the road formed an opposing line of battle, then advanced into the field north of the turnpike and returned the Confederate fire. Union guns were trotted up and put into action. At close range, without charging or retreating, the opposing lines fired again and again. The fighting lasted as long as there was light to see. In the dark Jackson's troops withdrew into the woods and the Union column, nearly a third of its men killed or wounded, moved off toward Manassas.

Jackson's position was at last known, and Pope ordered the Federal army to mass on the Warrenton Turnpike near Bull Run. Pope boasted that "we can bag the whole crowd" if his troops acted fast enough. Even the Federal units to the west that were blocking Lee's efforts to join Jackson were pulled back to head off and attack Jackson — a move that allowed Lee to advance with 30,000 men. As Pope tried to martial his forces, some Federal units had their orders changed for the third or fourth time in twenty-four hours. One Union general, revising his written instructions to his subordinates, asked an aide from Pope's headquarters how to spell "chaos." The aid told him and wrote later in his diary that he considered the question most timely.

Meanwhile, Jackson's troops had occupied a strong position along an unfinished railroad north of the Warrenton Turnpike. The alternating cuts and fills served as a trench and bulwark (as can be seen today). The Confederate line stretched for about two miles along the railroad bed, from Bull Run westward. The entire position was obscured by woods, which extended far to the rear and a short distance to the front.

Pope was anxious to crush Jackson before Lee arrived, and on August 29 he opened the attack before most of the scattered Union divisions were in position. First Pope sent a corps of 11,000 men straight against the center of Jackson's line. The Union guns shelled the woods, then the infantry advanced into thick fire. As the Federals entered the woods and approached the railroad, their ranks disintegrated and the attack lost momentum. Some Union troops reached the embankment and drove the Confederates farther into the woods, but a counterattack pushed the Yankees back. Pope refused a request from his corps commander to withdraw, and so the Federals remained along the fringe of the woods, firing ineffectively at the well-protected Southerners.

Pope sent more columns into battle as they reached the front. All told, about 20,000 Union soldiers assaulted the eastern end of the Confederate line near Sudley Springs, but their attacks came piecemeal, one after another. Six times various Federal units advanced, but the Confederates hung on and with desperate effort repulsed each of the Union attacks, which continued until dusk.

Pope also ordered an attack on the western end of the Confederate line, but the assault never occured. Approaching from Manassas, Brigadier General Fitz-John Porter disregarded orders and held back his corps. An officer in McClellan's Army of the Potomac, Porter detested Pope. He thought (perhaps correctly) that confusion reigned at Pope's headquarters. In any case, large clouds of dust to Porter's front convinced him that he was opposed by a strong enemy force. In fact, the dust was raised by J.E.B. Stuart's cavalry, which had been directed to create a stir and the illusion of superior strength. For his disobedience, Porter was court-martialed and cashiered from the army, but later reinstated. General Lee, who had just arrived and was organizing his forces, recalled after the war that Porter's troops were "peaceable looking." Still other Federal detachments failed to engage the enemy because of confusion. In all, nearly 30,000 soldiers, about half the Federal force, did no fighting on the 29th.

An equal number of Confederates were held out of the battle. Lee had reached Jackson's rear at midday, and during the early afternoon Major General James Longstreet, commander of the newly-arrived Confederate corps, massed his men to the west, just below the Warrenton Turnpike. Lee wanted to attack, but Longstreet recommended waiting and was allowed to have his way.

By the morning of August 30, Pope believed that he was on the verge of victory. His aide noted that on the previous evening "Pope was firmly of the opinion that Jackson was beaten and would get off during the night." The Confederates near Sudley Springs, after repulsing the Union attacks, had in fact withdrawn after dark, but only a small distance in order to shorten their line. One of Longstreet's divisions had advanced along the Warrenton Turnpike, skirmished briefly, and also withdrawn at dusk, convincing Pope that the Confederates had begun a nighttime retreat. The next morning Pope wrote to General Henry Halleck that on the 28th he had fought the combined forces of the enemy, adding, "The news just reaches me from the front that the enemy is retreating toward the mountains. I go forward at once to see."

Pope ordered his army to pursue the enemy, but more than half the day passed before his marching columns were organized. At mid-afternoon on the 30th, the Union army started west on the turnpike and in parallel lines to the north and south. The northern column, however, almost immediately encountered resistance, as strong as ever, along the unfinished railroad. Pope again attacked with wave after wave of troops. "As one line was repulsed another took its place and pressed forward as if determined by force of numbers and fury of assault to drive us from our positions," Jackson reported afterward. Union forces along the turnpike and to the south were, in part, sent north against the railroad. Thrusting with bayonets and swinging their guns like clubs, the opposing troops fought hand-to-hand. At the Deep Cut, the Confederates ran out of ammunition and resorted to throwing rocks. As the battle hung in the balance, Jackson sent word to Lee that he could not hold his ground without help.

Contacted by Lee, Longstreet sent a division to Jackson, and also massed eighteen field guns where the Warrenton Turnpike crosses a hill since called Battery Heights. This was the same stretch of road where Jackson had opened the battle two days earlier by attacking a passing Union column. Now Longstreet's artillery raked the lines of Union soldiers who were advancing across the field of fire toward the railroad. The Federals fell back in confusion, leaving the troops who had already reached the railroad to fend for themselves. Then Lee ordered a counterattack, and Longstreet's entire corps of 30,000 infantry moved forward south of the turnpike. The Union forces there had been stripped of many units to aid the attack on Jackson, and the Federal position crumbled. Two regiments of New York Zouaves tried to stop the Confederates, and although they slowed Longstreet's advance, they suffered some of the heaviest casualties of the war. (Two stone monuments at New York Avenue mark the location of this action.) Jackson's forces joined the attack, pressing forward from the northwest.

Grossly deceived — perhaps self-deceived — about the state of the battle, Pope nonetheless managed to salvage his army and to avoid a rout. He moved troops south of the turnpike to grapple with Longstreet's corps during the late afternoon and evening. The Federals tried to hold at Chinn Ridge, west of Sudley Road, but they were pushed back to Bald Hill and Henry Hill, where they made a stand at dusk. The Confederates were stopped, and as darkness fell the fighting died down.

During the night the Union forces retreated across Bull Run to Centreville, where they were joined by troops advancing from Alexandria. The reinforcements were from McClellan's Army of the Potomac, and according to one of Pope's officers, McClellan's men "greeted us with mocking laughter, taunts and jeers on the advantages of the new route to Richmond; while many of them in plain English expressed their joy at the downfall of the braggart rival of the great soldier of the peninsula."

On September 1 another, much smaller battle was fought near the estate of Chantilly a few miles north of Centreville. Two Federal divisions engaged Jackson's troops, who were attempting to advance in a wide circle around the Union camp. After an inconclusive fight in a thunderstorm, the Confederates drew back. The next day the Union army abandoned Centreville and retreated to Washington. Three thousand wounded Federals were evacuated by wagon and train. All told, the Union had lost 15,500 killed, wounded, and missing during two weeks of fighting in northern Virginia. The Confederates suffered more than 9,000 casualties, but were soon reinforced to an equal extent. Although still outnumbered by the Federal army, Lee's forces had regained control of northern Virginia and now threatened the Federal capital.

To the immense gratification of the officers and troops of the Army of the Potomac, McClellan was placed in command of the defense of Washington. Pope's demoralized army was merged with McClellan's, and Pope himself was sent out of the way to Minnesota. Within the government, many high officials were dissatisfied — even disgusted — with McClellan also. Lincoln himself had complained that McClellan seemed to want Pope to fail. But for at least the time being McClellan was needed. He alone elicited the devotion and enthusiasm of the many officers he had appointed and of the troops who served under them. On September 22 McClellan wrote from Washington to his wife that General Halleck was "begging me to help him out of his scrape and take command here," and that he had had "a pretty plain talk with him & Abe — a still plainer one this evening. The result is that I have reluctantly consented to take command here & try to save the capital."

McClellan was told to prepare the army for a campaign against Lee. "There is every probability that the enemy . . . will cross the Potomac, and make a raid into Maryland or Pennsylvania," Halleck wrote. "A moveable army must be immediately organized to meet him again in the field." Organization was McClellan's forte, and Lincoln reported a few days later that McClellan was "working like a beaver" at consolidating the existing forces, assigning recruits and miscellaneous units, and re-establishing an effective commissary and a coherent command structure. He had little time, for on September 5 the Confederate army forded the Potomac near Leesburg. Less than two weeks later, on September 17, the opposing armies collided again, this time at Antietam Creek near Sharpsburg, where more men died than in any other single day of the Civil War. (For a discussion of the battle of Antietam, see Chapter 18.)

AUTOMOBILE: From Exit 9 of the Capital Beltway (I-495) west of Arlington, follow Route 66 west about 17 miles to Route 234 north for Manassas National Battlefield Park. The visitor center, which is on the right off Route 234 about 0.7 mile from Route 66, provides a good overview of the first and second battles of Manassas. However, the Second Manassas Hiking Trail starts at the picnic area on the west side of Route 234 a mile north of the visitor center. There are two parking lots for the picnic area: an upper lot bordering the road and a lower lot at the end of a driveway. If you can, park in the lower lot, where the trail starts.

WALK: Except toward the end, the route described below follows the Second Manassas Hiking Trail, which is marked by occasional green crosses.

From the picnic area at the lower parking lot, the trail starts as a worn path leading about 40 yards to the right of a small, concrete-block restroom (i.e., in a line that forms an imaginary extension of the road that leads to the parking lot). Cross a meadow, pass through a hedgerow, and follow a lane straight along the edge of a field. (Yellow blazes mark a horse trail which at times follows the same route as the Second Manassas Hiking Trail.) Continue into the woods and straight past an intersection where the horse trail turns to the left. Follow the hiking trail to a small parking lot.

From the parking lot, continue half-left across a road intersection and into the woods on a footpath that follows the unfinished railroad where Stonewall Jackson established his line of defense. (In addition to green crosses, there are red blazes that mark a short loop.) Pass the "dump" of rock that was to have been used to build the railroad grade and bridge abutments at a small stream; continue along the railbed to the monument at the Deep Cut.

At the Deep Cut, a spur of the green-cross trail leads 0.8 mile to Battery Heights. To follow the spur trail, continue straight along the railroad bed. Cross a stream and continue on the raised roadbed for about 140 yards, then turn left to follow the green-cross trail away from the railroad. Cross a meadow and continue through woods and open fields to the cannons at Battery Heights. Return to the monument at the Deep Cut by the way you came.

To continue on the main circuit from the monument at the Deep Cut, follow the green (and red) blazes away from the railroad bed and along a broad, grassy swath through the woods. Bear half-right on the green-cross trail where the red-blazed path leads left. Follow a rivulet through the meadow, then turn left across the stream. Climb to a rail fence bordering a road. With caution, cross the road and turn right onto a path marked by green (and yellow) blazes. With a rail fence on the left, follow the path parallel with the road. Cross a small stream on a wooden pedestrian bridge and continue along the rail fence to an intersection with Lee Highway.

At Lee Highway turn left. With the highway and a rail fence on the right, walk downhill and across a small bridge and up to a parking lot and Groveton Confederate Cemetery. From the cemetery continue about 100 yards downhill along Lee Highway. With care, turn right across the highway at an intersection with a park road called New York Avenue. Walking on the left shoulder of the road, follow New York Avenue to a loop near two monuments to the Duryee and National Zouaves, whose regiments suffered heavy casualties in an effort to stop the counterattack by Longstreet's corps on the afternoon of August 30.

To the right of the National Zouave monument, pick up the green (and yellow and orange) blazes leading downhill into the woods. Cross a pedestrian bridge over Youngs Branch, then turn right upstream, passing an intersection where the orange trail leads left away from the stream. Go 40 yards upstream along Youngs Branch, then bear left uphill. After half a mile, the trail reaches a gravel and dirt road intersecting from the left. Turn left and follow the gravel and dirt road, eventually reaching a gate by an asphalt park road. Continue straight along the ridge next to the road (although first you may want to make a short detour downhill to the right to examine the foundations of the Chinn House and the remains of the Houe family cemetery).

Follow the park road along the top of the grassy ridge. At a loop at the end of the road, continue straight across a meadow in a line parallel with the edge of the woods on the left. (By now you have left the green-cross trail.) Pass through a gap in a hedgerow, then turn right downhill. (Note occasional blue blazes on the trees to the right.) Near the bottom of the slope, follow a flight of stairs downhill, then cross a small stream. Continue diagonally across the next field to the intersection of Lee Highway and Route 234 (Sudley Road).

At the road intersection, turn left. Follow the grassy shoulder next to Lee Highway 200 yards. Opposite a group of historic markers, turn right and carefully cross the road. (From here on, there is no set path.) Continue straight uphill away from Lee Highway and through a meadow, with hedgerows to either side. Climb straight to the crest of the ridge. Sudley Road and the entrance to the parking lots where the walk began are to the right.

7

THE WASHINGTON & OLD DOMINION RAILROAD REGIONAL PARK

Walking, bicycling, or ski touring — up to 30 miles (48.3 kilometers) round trip. From Herndon to Leesburg (or vice versa) along an old railroad that now forms a hiker's highway through open country. The ties and rails have been removed and the trail paved with finely crushed stone and asphalt. Although the route serves as a right-of-way for the transmission lines of the Virginia Electric Power Company, the pylons and wires simply reinforce the marching, cross-country linearity of this unique park. If you do not want to retrace your steps, a car shuttle is necessary. For a shorter walk, start or stop at the village of Ashburn, about half way between Herndon and Leesburg. Managed by the Northern Virginia Regional Park Authority (703) 352-5900.

A HIKER-BIKER TRAIL extends from the Potomac River just below Washington National Airport northwest for about forty-five miles through Falls Church, Vienna, Reston, Herndon, and Leesburg to the rural town of Purcellville, nine miles short of the Blue Ridge. For the most part the trail follows the former roadbed of the Washington & Old Dominion Railroad, but it also uses the Wayne F. Anderson Bikeway in Alexandria and the Four Mile Run Trail in Arlington. Endurance specialists may want to hike the

entire distance, but only a shorter excursion along the most scenic part of the railroad trail is recommended here.

A brief review of the entire railroad trail is as follows: the portion between the Potomac River and Falls Church is citified and frequently disrupted by roads and highways, but there are pleasant sections along Four Mile Run south of Route 66. Between Falls Church and Herndon, the trail is more attractive, but somewhat crowded by suburbia. The fifteen miles between Herndon and Leesburg is the best part, and this is the section described below in the directions. Although suburban development impinges on the old rail line for two or three miles west of Herndon, the countryside is mostly farmland and woods. For mile after mile the route follows the roadbed along cuts and atop elevated embankments, at one point crossing the high bridge at Goose Creek. Finally, west of Leesburg the trail deteriorates. Although passable on foot, this last section is not recommended here, since the trail is interrupted or bordered at intervals by major roads and highways. For a description and series of maps covering the entire W & OD Railroad Regional Park and connecting bicycle paths between the Potomac River and Purcellville, a trail guide is available from the Northern Virginia Regional Park Authority.

The Washington & Old Dominion Railroad stopped running in 1968, after more than 110 years of operation under at least eight names and almost as many corporate owners. During its life the line hauled farm products, soldiers and supplies during the Civil War, tourists going to and from the Blue Ridge, commuters, and freight for local industries, earning as its nickname, because of its desultory service, the "Virginia Creeper."

Construction of a railroad westward from tidewater on the Potomac was first proposed by a group of Alexandria merchants and bankers concerned about the eclipse of their city by the rival port of Baltimore, through which flowed a lucrative and growing trade with the Ohio Valley. Baltimore was the eastern terminus of the nation's first commercial railroad, the Baltimore & Ohio, which by 1840 already had demonstrated its superiority to the

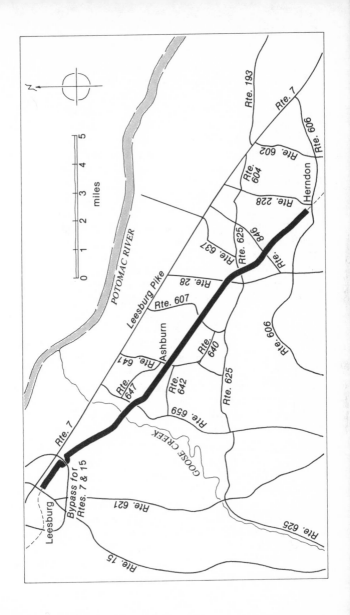

Chesapeake & Ohio Canal, until then the chief hope of the Potomac ports of Georgetown and Alexandria. Accordingly, early in 1847 the Virginia General Assembly chartered the Alexandria & Harpers Ferry Railroad Company. At Harpers Ferry the proposed line would join the Winchester & Potomac Railroad, already serving the Shenandoah Valley. The plan, however, attracted little support, especially after 1848, when the Shenandoah commerce was diverted to Baltimore by a junction with the B & O at Harpers Ferry.

In 1853 the Virginia legislature amended the charter of the stillborn railroad by specifying a new route running from Alexandria through Leesburg and across the Blue Ridge to the coal fields of Hampshire County (later incorporated into West Virginia). The enterprise was rechristened the Alexandria, Loudon & Hampshire Railroad Company. Again, however, the promoters had trouble attracting capital, and it was not until the Commonwealth of Virginia undertook to buy three shares of stock for every two purchased by other investors that the company obtained the money to survey the line, compensate owners whose land was condemned for the right-of-way, and begin construction. Between 1855 and 1859, the roadbed was graded from Alexandria to Clarke's Gap west of Leesburg, and a single track laid down as far as Herndon. The ties were white oak, used at the rate of 2,700 per mile. Although the contractors agreed to take 25 percent of the company's stock as part of their payment, progress was slowed nonetheless by lack of cash. In May 1860, service was established once a day each way — later increased to twice a day — for the two-hour, 38-mile trip between Alexandria and Leesburg.

The line had not been in operation more than a year before it was devastated by the Civil War. On May 24, 1861, a few weeks after Virginia had seceded from the Union, Federal forces crossed the Potomac River and seized Alexandria and its various railroad terminals. In response, Confederate troops tore up the tracks and burned bridges along the line to Leesburg, so that the section west of Vienna remained useless throughout the war. East of Vienna, however, the line was operated by the Federals as part of the U.S.

Military Railroads. Thousands of Yankees camped along the tracks in the vicinity of Four Mile Run, which became so polluted with soap from Union wash that the train engineers complained that their locomotive boilers, when filled with water from the stream, frothed with suds.

Lewis McKenzie, president of the Alexandria, Loudoun and Hampshire Railroad, was a Unionist who posted Federal flags on his locomotives the day Alexandria was taken — unlike the pro-Southern president of the Alexandria & Washington Railroad, who transferred his engines to another line and sent them to the Confederacy. McKenzie urged the War Department in Washington to repair his railroad and even to extend it westward. That failing, he asked that the line be released from Federal control, but instead it was retained for the use of the Union army longer than any other Virginia railroad.

After the war the railroad company slowly repaired the line. During the course of 1866 and '67, service was reintroduced at Herndon, Sterling, Ashburn, and Leesburg as bridges were rebuilt, including the 278-foot span at Goose Creek. In 1870 West Virginia authorized the railroad to extend its line to the Ohio River, and the company optimistically changed its name to the Washington & Ohio Railroad. The company already had borrowed heavily by issuing corporate bonds paying 7 percent interest; now the capital stock was expanded and then expanded again. By the end of 1874 the track reached Round Hill west of Purcellville, and grading had begun on the roadbed toward Winchester, beyond the Blue Ridge. This objective, however, was never reached. Burdened by its huge construction debt, the railroad sank into bankruptcy, and a receiver was appointed at the beginning of 1878.

In 1882 the railroad's entire property was sold to a new corporation, which promptly collapsed. The next year, the railroad again changed hands and names. Then, in 1886, the line came under the control of a rival railroad company that wanted to put an end — and did — to the plans to extend the line west of the Blue Ridge.

In 1894 the railroad emerged from a period of financial confusion when it was acquired by the newly-chartered Southern Railway Company, which in 1900 extended the tracks to Bluemont at the foot of the Blue Ridge. By being part of the Southern's vast system, the line benefited from a rail link into Washington. Operating as the Bluemont Branch of the Southern Railway, the road for the first time did a good business, carrying vacationing families, hunters, and fishermen to the numerous boarding houses and summer hotels that were popular in Loudon County. Among others, President Grover Cleveland is said to have taken the train often to Leesburg to fish in Tuscarora Creek.

In 1911 the Southern Railway leased the Bluemont Branch to the Washington & Old Dominion Railway Company. The W & OD already ran a newly-constructed trolley line from Washington to Great Falls, and it soon electrified the Bluemont Branch as well. The new company continued to promote the tourist traffic, publishing in 1916 a booklet entitled *Resorts *** From the Capital to the Blue Ridge on the Washington and Old Dominion Railway,* extolling the inexpensive accommodations and cooling breezes to be found only a short trainride away from the summertime miasma of Washington. The price of a round-trip ticket between the capital and Bluemont was a dollar. Despite the amenities and low cost, however, passenger revenue fell from 1919 onward as automobiles became commonplace. The railroad steadily lost money, and in 1932, when the shareholders refused to meet further deficits, the line again went into receivership.

The receivers drastically reduced services and expenses. The Great Falls Branch was abandoned, and later everything west of Purcellville. In 1935 a new corporation was formed with a slightly different name — the Washington & Old Dominion Railroad — and bought the leasehold rights, rolling stock, and other assets of the old company for a mere $35,000. The reborn railroad negotiated a new lease with the Southern Railway at a greatly reduced rent. Unable to afford the cost of repairing its system of overhead wires, the company converted to diesel locomotives. Passenger service was terminated, but freight revenues rose.

The advent of World War II brought sudden prosperity to the line. In 1942 freight revenue reached $335,503, which was 2½ times greater than three years earlier. Gasoline rationing restricted the use of automobiles, and so passenger service — ordered as an emergency measure by the Office of Defense Transportation — was resumed and for a period proved profitable. In 1945 the company managed to buy the line outright from the Southern Railway for only $70,000, the equivalent of less than two years' rent. Passenger service was again terminated in 1951. Four years later the company had only sixty-nine employees, but its revenues were at an all time high of $545,452. In 1956 the shareholders sold the line to the Chesapeake & Ohio Railroad for about $445,000 of C & O stock.

The line's future, however, remained doubtful. Throughout the newly-suburbanized region of northern Virginia, a process of de-industrialization was occurring as higher land values and restrictive zoning forced many businesses to leave the area. The railroad nonetheless prospered for a few years in the late 1950s during the construction of Dulles International Airport, which required immense quantities of sand for the concrete runways. But when the new town of Reston was begun in 1961, the railroad received virtually no business from the project, despite the fact that the line passed through the town; instead, trucks hauled in almost all materials for the new community. At the same time the Virginia Highway Department condemned a spur of the line for part of Route 66 and other road projects near Rosslyn, where many of the railroad's industrial customers were located.

The final blow came when the Virginia Electric Power Company, in a transaction that used the state's Department of Highways as an intermediary — and according to some, as a screen to conceal what really was going on — agreed to buy almost all of the railroad's right-of-way for an undisclosed price (but at least $3.5 million) if the State Corporation Commission of Virginia and the Interstate Commerce Commission approved the railroad's petition to abandon the line. In 1968, over the objection of several local governments and business groups, the petition was approved and the trains stopped running. Nine years later, the Virginia Electric Power Company sold the roadbed, subject to an easement for its power lines, to the Northern Virginia Regional Park Authority.

AUTOMOBILE: Four access points — Herndon, Route 28, Ashburn, and Leesburg — are described below. Other access points where roads cross the path are evident from the map.

To reach Herndon from the Capital Beltway (1-495) northwest of Arlington, take Exit 10 for Route 7 (Leesburg Pike) west toward Tysons Corner. (A bypass is contemplated for Tysons Corner, which may affect these directions and some of the specified distances.) Follow Route 7 west about 7 miles to an intersection with Route 606 west, then turn left and follow Route 606 for 4 miles to an intersection with Lynn Street on the right in the center of Herndon. The railroad station and path are located next to Lynn Street under high electric transmission lines.

By starting at Route 28, you can avoid the suburban development that sprawls west for two or three miles from Herndon. From the Capital Beltway, follow Route 7 west almost 15 miles, then turn left onto Route 28 and go 2.3 miles to a point where the railroad path crosses the road under high electric transmission lines. Park in a lot west of the road.

To reach Ashburn by automobile, follow Route 7 to an intersection with Route 641, located about 18 miles west of the Capital Beltway. Turn left onto Route 641 and go 1.9 miles to the point where the railroad path crosses the road under high electric transmission lines. Park in a lot on the left.

To reach Leesburg by automobile, follow Route 7 more than 23 miles west from the Capital Beltway. As you approach Leesburg, use the left-hand lane to

*continue straight into town on Business Route 7. Turn
left onto King Street (Business Route 15), then go 3½
blocks to the point where the railroad path crosses
King Street just beyond a small bridge.*

*WALK: It is possible, of course, to follow the railroad
path either west or east. If you start at the former train
station in Herndon, head west across Station Street,
leaving the old station behind on the left. Pass a golf
course near the edge of Herndon; continue past
suburban development at Sterling Park before reaching
the open country and the village of Ashburn. Between
Ashburn and Leesburg, the main landmark is the high
bridge at Goose Creek. At the bypass for Routes 7 and
15 outside Leesburg, follow the path as it detours left
under the highway, then back to the former railroad
bed. Continue into Leesburg, staying on the railroad
path all the way to King Street, which crosses the trail
next to a small concrete bridge with two arches.*

*If you begin at King Street in Leesburg, the small
stream of Town Run is on the left for the first 125 yards
as you start east. Outside of town, detour downhill to
the right and under the highway where Routes 7 and 15
bypass Leesburg. Cross the high bridge at Goose
Creek and continue east to Ashburn and Herndon.*

8

DRANESVILLE DISTRICT PARK

*Walking — 3 miles (4.8 kilometers). Follow Scotts Run
downstream to a waterfall next to the Potomac River, then
continue along the heights and bluffs of the Potomac
Palisades. Return through wooded ravines and upland. This
park, which offers some of the best scenery and walking near
Washington, would have been a housing subdivision but for
the efforts of local citizens. Open daily from dawn until dusk.
Managed by the Fairfax County Park Authority (703)
941-5000.*

A 1969 PLAT for the 336-acre tract of woods, ravines, and
Potomac Palisades that now forms Dranesville District Park shows
a subdivision plan, complete with curving drives, cul-de-sacs, and
lots for 309 houses clustered along the ridges. The plan was
sweetened (for consumption by Fairfax County officials and local
residents) by a pathway and strip of land comprising twenty-six
acres along Scotts Run and the Potomac River, to be dedicated to
public use. Because the lots were approximately half an acre each,
much of the land along the ravines and river bluff would have been
excess, titled in a homeowners' association and left undistrubed,
but in other respects the subdivision would have resembled the
conventional developments that can be seen on adjacent tracts
between Georgetown Pike and the Potomac. Just how the entire
336-acre property became instead a public park preserved in a
natural state is an instructive story.

Before the subdivision was proposed and the counter-crusade
for a park began, the property was the wooded weekend estate of

Edward B. Burling, one of the founders of the Washington law firm of Covington and Burling. Burling had a small cabin at the crest of the bluff, where he regularly invited his friends and acquaintances for Sunday lunch. His guests included many of the top government figures and political thinkers of the 1930s, '40s, and '50s, and his cabin was a sort of rustic *salon*. Burling did not mind if others hiked on his land or waded in Scotts Run in his absence, and so the tract served as an unofficial park and nature preserve for the neighborhood, reinforcing the area's tone of low-keyed, woodsy exclusiveness.

Burling died in 1966, and three years later one of the region's largest developers, Miller & Smith Associates, Inc., contracted to buy the land from the Burling family trust, but the sale was contingent on county approval for Miller & Smith's subdivision plan. Submitted in the spring of 1969, the plan was approved, in most respects, by Fairfax County's professional planning staff, but local residents appealed the matter to the county planning commission. Miller & Smith also appealed, seeking approval of an aspect of their plan that entailed relocating the route for the extension of the George Washington Memorial Parkway. Everyone knew that it was highly unlikely that the parkway ever would be extended outside the Capital Beltway, but plats of future roads showed the parkway running across the middle of the Burling tract, and Miller & Smith wanted the route moved to the southern edge of the property, and even, in part, shifted onto neighboring land. And so began what newspaper accounts came to call, as the issues developed, a "heated controversy," a "battle," a "donnybrook," and a "revolution."

According to an account in the Washington *Star* for November 3, 1969, "The revolutionaries, ironically, are the establishment this time. They're the doctors, lawyers, merchants, and chiefs of the 'Gold Coast' area in and around McLean, Va.—the people who care about open space and who have the wherewithal to live in it." Organized into a group called the Georgetown Pike and Potomac River Association, the neighborhood residents conceded that the Miller & Smith plan was far above average (as such plans go) in

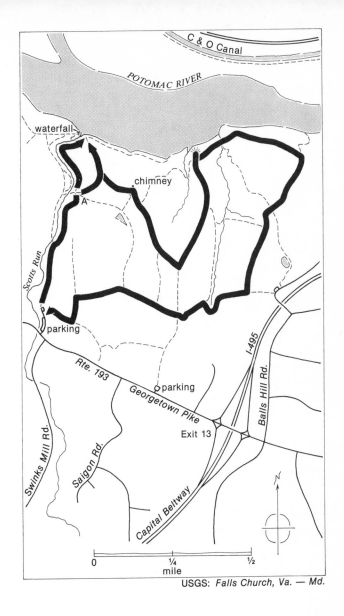

waterfall

chimney

A

Scotts Run

parking

Rte. 193

parking

Georgetown Pike

I-495

Balls Hill Rd.

Exit 13

Swinks Mill Rd.

Saigon Rd.

Capital Beltway

C & O Canal

POTOMAC RIVER

N

0   1/4   1/2
mile

USGS: *Falls Church, Va. — Md.*

adapting to the difficult terrain and in preserving wooded slopes, but they asserted that the development nonetheless would create massive erosion and sedimentation, and that the number of lots should be reduced to about a hundred. The planning commission responded by referring the matter to the regional soil and water conservation agency for review. Pressing simultaneously for public acquisition of the land, opponents of the subdivision also managed to attract the interest of the Northern Virginia Regional Park Authority and the Fairfax County Park Authority, which were given the opportunity to consider whether the Burling tract should be placed on the Fairfax County Public Facilities Plan as a park site.

The developers, however, had not yet begun to fight. They pledged to use "the most modern soil erosion techniques that responsible people can devise," and their consultants prepared an erosion and sedimentation control plan that a county official called "the best that has been submitted to the county as of this date." The Northern Virginia Park Authority also endorsed the plan after Miller & Smith agreed to give the park authority not only twenty-six acres along Scotts Run and the Potomac River, but also a first option to buy twenty-seven choice lots atop the bluff overlooking the Potomac. The Fairfax County Park Authority acquiesced in this arrangement.

As local agencies moved closer to approving the subdivision plan, the park partisans received a boost from the Federal government. After visits by several prominent residents of the Burling area, Secretary of the Interior Walter J. Hickel wrote to the Fairfax County Planning Commission that his department was "interested in this remarkable piece of land." He followed up with an extraordinary offer to pay half the cost of buying the property, up to $1.5 million, using money from his department's contingency fund (the largest such grant ever), but the governor of Virginia and county officials said that the state and local governments could not afford to match the Federal offer. Efforts to raise matching funds from the Nature Conservancy and private foundations were stymied by lack of interest among local public officials.

Matters dragged on, but by early March 1970, the struggle appeared to be going irreversibly against the park proponents. One headline declared, "Conservationists Beat on Burling." The Fairfax County Planning Commission finally granted a qualified approval of the subdivision plan, and, on appeal, so did the Fairfax County Board of Supervisors. Although the matter of the route for the George Washington Memorial Parkway was still unresolved, no legal barrier remained to prevent Miller & Smith from beginning construction on the first phase of the project. But the developers hesitated and returned to the supervisors a month later for a ruling on the parkway relocation.

The second hearing before the Board of Supervisors was a turning point. After being innundated by a torrent of testimony in support of the park and presented with a park petition containing 2,300 signatures collected door-to-door by high school students, the supervisors requested the county park authority to advise them whether the Burling tract would be suitable for a Dranesville Magisterial District Park (each district elects a supervisor) for which $600,000 of county funds already had been authorized by a 1966 bond referendum.

As the tide of battle shifted toward those fighting for a park, the controversy began to get ugly. In letters to newspapers and even in some editorials, proponents of the park were called snobs who were trying to raid the county treasury in order to keep more residents out of their neighborhood. Student activists, whose interest in a park had been sparked by their parents and by classroom discussions and presentations in the schools, were termed an undoctrinated and unruly mob. The supervisor representing the Dranesville District accused the park advocates, whom she called "a few nearby property owners zealously guarding against new neighbors," of "concealment or distortion of some of the basic facts" about costs, taxes, and the loss of opportunity to buy parkland at other sites that she favored. The Georgetown Pike and Potomac River Association in turn alleged that the deliberations and negative decision of the Northern Virginia Regional Park Authority had been tainted by glaring conflicts of interest by some members of its board who had business ties with the developers, and that Miller & Smith had greatly inflated the number of allowable clustered houselots by counting land allocated to the George Washington Memorial Parkway or that was often flooded or otherwise undevelopable.

At the meeting of the Fairfax County Park Authority on April 29, 1970, the movement for a park gathered momentum. By a margin of four to one, speakers favored buying the Burling tract, and the owner of a large property nearby offered to loan the park authority $1.5 million for three years at 5 percent interest to make the purchase. A few days later the park authority recommended acquisition of the land to the Board of Supervisors, who eventually decided to hold a referendum among Dranesville District voters on whether they were willing to be taxed additionally to raise $1.5 million toward buying the Burling property.

As the date for the referendum approached, attention was focused on the cost to each taxpayer — about $80 for the average homeowner, according to one county official. The local Chamber of Commerce campaigned against the park, objecting to the extra taxes that would be levied on business property. A few large landowners also objected, saying that they would be taxed far more than most, and that they were already, in effect, providing open space for the community free of charge (but failing to point out that the public had no right of access to their large estates and horsefarms, and that low taxes were a hidden subsidy of their holding costs until the day they sold their land for huge profits, as some have). Other opponents pointed out that the cost of the Burling tract was likely to be higher than anticipated, and that the development of part of it for even a few public tennis courts, ballfields, a swimming pool, and a nature center (as was talked of) would cost still more money. It was said that the community's need for ballfields would probably entail the purchase of more land elsewhere, since only a small part of the Burling tract is level. Proponents of the park countered that the availability of Federal funds was an extraordinary opportunity that should not be lost, and that the development of the land for houses would itself lead to higher taxes because each additional suburban family typically requires more in government services than its newly-constructed home yields in tax revenue.

After a campaign in which numerous students distributed leaflets door-to-door urging purchase of the land for a park, voters of the Dranesville District approved the special tax. Two weeks later, in a confrontation designed to force speedy negotiations about the terms of sale, the developers sent their bulldozers to the site and began clearing a road through the woods — a move the park proponents termed "bulldozer blackmail." Carrying signs and singing "This Land is Our Land," dozens of youngsters and mothers picketed the entrance to the property. The fracas ended abruptly when Miller & Smith agreed to sell the land to the county for $3.6 million (they had bought it a few months earlier for $2.4 million), provided the price was paid by September 4. For a period there was doubt whether the money could be raised that quickly, but the governor of Virginia agreed to contribute $300,000 of Federal funds earmarked for the state, and the rest of the local share was borrowed on a short-term basis.

There was still some unpleasantness after the Burling tract was purchased. A few residents of Dranesville District filed a suit alleging technical irregularities in the referendum and complaining that Dranesville was being specially taxed to create a county facility, but their case eventually failed. Others complained of trash left by fishermen and teenagers. Some called the park a "green-tinged white elephant" that was redundant and useless because of other large parks along the Potomac. After you have been to Dranesville District Park, you may want to consider how you would have sided in the controversy over the Burling tract, and what (if anything) you are willing to do for the preservation of similar areas in your own community.

AUTOMOBILE: From Exit 13 of the Capital Beltway (I-495) northwest of McLean, take Route 193 (Georgetown Pike) toward Great Falls. Follow Route 193 a little more than 0.5 mile to a parking lot for

Dranesville District Park on the right, next to Scotts
Run and opposite the intersection with Swinks Mill
Road.

There is a plan, however, to close the parking lot by
Scotts Run and to enlarge a small lot located closer to
the beltway. If the lot by Scotts Run is indeed closed,
park in the other lot and use the map to join the route
described below.

WALK: From the gate at the back of the parking lot next
to Scotts Run, follow a path gradually downhill. Where
the main path fords Scotts Run, veer right along the
bank on a narrow footpath. (Although this trail is not as
inviting as the wider path, it avoids the need to ford
back across Scotts Run farther downstream, where the
water is deeper.)

With Scotts Run on the left, continue downstream on
the narrow footpath. At times the trail crosses eroded
slopes. Continue as the path veers half-right away from
the stream, then half-left to a trail junction with a wide
path next to Scotts Run. From this point (marked A on
the map), those who feel confident of their ability to do
a little scrambling can continue downstream, eventually
passing above a waterfall where Scotts Run empties
into the Potomac River. A more conservative way to
reach the waterfall and the Potomac from point A is to
go half-right uphill on a wide path; after following a cut
across the top of the ridge, curve left downhill past a
trail intersecting from the right. Descend to the
Potomac River next to the mouth of Scotts Run.

From the waterfall at the mouth of Scotts Run, head
uphill on a wide path. (If you approached the waterfall
by the conservative route described above, you came
by this path.) As you near the crest of the slope, fork
left and continue uphill to a chimney that marks the site
of Edward Burling's cabin. Turn right and continue on a

wide path, with the terrain sloping downhill on both sides. After about 0.3 mile (where the path takes an abrupt turn half-right), turn very sharply left onto a less worn trail. Follow this trail for 0.4 mile to a bluff above the Potomac River. Continue downhill to a crag overlooking Stubblefield Falls, as the rapids are called.

About 40 yards uphill from the rocky overlook above Stubblefield Falls, turn downstream onto a narrow footpath leading along the bluff. With the river downhill to the left, pass other crags. Descend over jumbled rocks and across a small stream. Continue gradually downhill, then up and along the hillside on the narrow footpath. At a T-intersection, turn right uphill.

At the top of the slope, continue straight through a four-way intersection and downhill. Pass a trail intersecting from the right. Continue more or less straight through the woods, then turn right at a T-intersection. Continue as the trail detours left around the head of a gully. At a T-intersection, turn left uphill. Pass straight through a junction with a wide path. Eventually, turn left at a T-intersection. Cross a rivulet at the bottom of a broad ravine, then turn right immediately at another T-intersection. With the rivulet toward the right, follow the path back to your starting point.

GREAT FALLS PARK, VIRGINIA

Walking — 4 miles (6.4 kilometers). Our local Niagara and Grand Canyon. From Great Falls trace the remains of George Washington's Patowmack Canal, built to implement his dream of converting the Potomac River into a waterway to the West. Continue downstream along the rim of Mather Gorge. The trail follows a bluff and ridge above the Potomac, then eventually descends into the deep ravine of Difficult Run. Return to Great Falls on an old carriage road. Other trails provide opportunities to cut short the route described here if it becomes too strenuous. Dogs must be leashed. The park is open daily from dawn until dusk. The visitor center is open daily, except Christmas, 9 A.M. to 5 P.M. Managed by the National Park Service (703) 759-2915.

PRESIDENT THEODORE ROOSEVELT, who often found time for hikes and rides in the vicinity of Washington, called Great Falls "the most beautiful place around here." Weaving its way in several channels through a wide swath of jagged rocks, the Potomac River drops nearly forty feet in two hundred yards, then enters a narrow gorge with vertical walls. Smaller rapids immediately above and below the main cataract create an overall fall of about seventy-five feet in a mile. The entire spectacle is best seen from the Virginia shore at points passed by this walk.

The Virginia shore at Great Falls also features relics of a little-known canal built before the Chesapeake & Ohio Canal was constructed along the Maryland side of the river in the second quarter of the nineteenth century. As early as 1772 the colonial

legislature of Virginia approved a bill, prepared by George Washington and Henry Lee, for improving navigation on the upper reaches of the Potomac. A similar bill was needed from Maryland, but the legislation failed to pass because of opposition from Baltimore. Baltimore merchants feared that the canal project would divert trade from their city, from which a wagon road ran west through Frederick and Fort Cumerland to the Ohio Valley, recently wrested from the French and now open to settlement.

Following the Revolutionary War, however, both Virginia and Maryland passed bills, at the urging of George Washington, authorizing the formation of a corporation to make the Potomac navigable from tidewater at Georgetown to the highest point possible on the river's north branch, but at least as far upstream as Fort Cumberland. Where feasible, a channel would be cleared in the river itself, allowing passage of shallow-draft boats, even during the dry season. The company was authorized to construct canals and locks around rapids and was granted powers of eminent domain to acquire the necessary land. The legislation specified an elaborate schedule of tolls based on the value of the cargo, with upward adjustments for bulky items. The governments of Virginia and Maryland subscribed for large blocks of stock. Other shares were purchased by many of the region's leading families, who hoped that the project would channel commerce through the ports of Georgetown and Alexandria, and, of course, earn a large income in tolls. Some boosters even predicted a 50 percent annual return on the investment. On May 17, 1885, the stockholders met at Alexandria to organize formally the Patowmack Company and to elect George Washington its president, a position he held for four years until he became President of the United States.

Washington had long been interested in development of the Potomac River, which he called "one of the finest Rivers in the world." In 1785 a visitor to Washington's home at Mount Vernon wrote in his diary, "The General sent the bottle about pretty freely after dinner, and gave success to the navigation of the Potomac for his toast, which he has very much at heart . . . ." On a personal level,

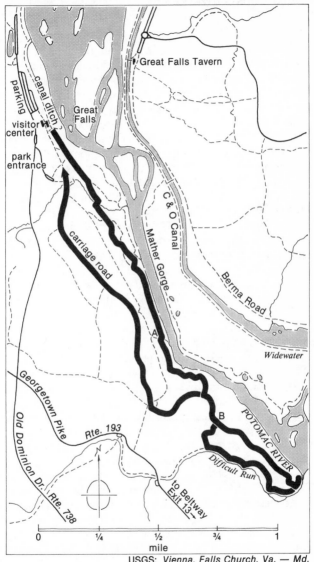

Great Falls Tavern

Great Falls

parking

canal ditch

visitor center

park entrance

carriage road

C & O Canal

Mather Gorge

Berma Road

A

Widewater

Georgetown Pike

Old Dominion Dr. Rte. 738

Rte. 193

B

POTOMAC RIVER

Difficult Run

to Beltway Exit 13

N

0 ¼ ½ ¾ 1
mile

USGS: *Vienna, Falls Church, Va. — Md.*

Washington had extensive land holdings in western Pennsylvania that would increase in value if communication with the seaboard could be improved. And apart from his investments, he was convinced that the Potomac was the best route to the West from the mid-Atlantic states. Saying that "there is nothing which binds ... one State to another but interest," he supported a number of canal and road projects that would increase commerce and inter-dependence among the former colonies and the Ohio Valley.

For three decades after its incorporation, the Patowmack Company struggled to bypass a series of major obstacles along the river and its tributaries. Five canals up to two miles long were built on the Potomac at Little Falls, Great Falls, Seneca Falls, and above and below Harpers Ferry. Short canals were also cut around rapids on the Shenandoah River and Antietam Creek, and improvements were made on other tributaries as well. The goal of making the river passable even during periods of low water did not prove feasible, but by an expenditure of $730,000, the Patowmack Company opened several hundred miles of river to navigation by small boats during favorable water conditions.

The biggest obstacle along the river was, of course, Great Falls, where the Patowmack Company built the Great Falls Skirting Canal. It had five lift locks and was 1,820 yards long. Above the falls a wing dam 400 yards long projected at an angle upstream into the river, gathering water into the canal. Spillways fed water to a gristmill and a forge midway along the canal. A large collecting basin provided a reservoir for operating the lift locks farther down the waterway and a place for boats to load and unload goods. Finally, a series of locks, the last three occupying a deep cleft blasted through the rock, conveyed boats to and from the gorge below. Although in an advanced state of ruin, many features of the canal are still visible.

Begun in 1786, most of the Great Falls Skirting Canal was excavated in one year, but the section containing the lift locks was not finished until 1802. Experienced engineers were hard to find, and a series of five men supervised the project. One route for the locks was abandoned, on the advice of an English consultant, after much time and money had been wasted. As late as 1797, when Leonard Harbaugh took over as chief engineer and superintendent, none of the locks had been completed. Harbaugh already had finished construction of the skirting canal around Little Falls, and he also carried the work at Great Falls through to completion, but not until after the company's funds were temporarily exhausted and work interrupted for two years. In 1798 the company obtained loans to finish the project, pledging shares of its own stock and even its future tolls as collateral. Of the five Potomac canals, the Great Falls project was the last to be finished, and for several years the area was a bottleneck where boats had to be unloaded and their cargo carried by wagon around the cataract. For a period barrels of flour and other commodities were rolled down an inclined plane to boats below.

Because of the shortage of workmen in eighteenth-century America, the Patowmack Company contracted for slaves and indentured laborers to dig the various skirting canals and clear the river. Virginia slave owners hired out their slaves for a yearly sum; clothes and rations were the obligation of the company, which also had to reimburse the owner if one of his slaves died. Indentured immigrants, who had agreed to work for a specified period for the person who paid their way to America, were hired from ships arriving in Baltimore and Philadelphia. Most of these men were Irish or German, and many attempted to avoid their obligations by running away. For example, on February 22, 1786, the *Maryland Chronicle* stated:

> From the *Alexandria Gazette* of the 1st January we hear that several servants who had purchased to work on the Patowmack Navigation lately ran away, but soon after being apprehended, were sentenced to have their heads and eyebrows shaved, which operation was immediately executed, and is to be continued every week during the time of their servitude, or until their behavior evinces that they are brought to a sense of their duty. This notice, it is expected, will sufficiently apprize the country should they again make a similar attempt.

Nonetheless, four months later the superintendent at Great Falls advertised that eight indentured servants, two of them shaved, had run off, and he offered a reward for their return.

During the summer of 1786, the Patowmack Company employed more than two hundred men, most of them at Great Falls. Some of the workers were skilled artisans, such as blacksmiths, wheelwrights, carpenters, and stone masons, paid by their output. Most, however, were laborers engaged in digging, hauling, drilling, and blasting. Apparently they were a rowdy lot, not above attacking and plundering the company wagons that brought in supplies. Work quotas were enforced by withholding the daily ration of rum (three-quarters pint for whites, less for slaves) from those who fell short of their assigned tasks. Working from seven in the morning until six in the evening and living in crude cabins and barracks, the laborers led a rough life. Some of the men had wives who were hired to do cooking, cleaning, and housekeeping for the camp. A report written by the superintendent on the subject of blasting powder reflects the atmosphere that prevailed at the Great Falls project:

> Great Falls, potowmack July 3rd 1786. Sir, We have Been much Imposed upon the past Two weeks in the powder way. (We had our Blowers, One run off, the other Blown up). We therefore was Obliged to have two new hands put to Blowing and there was much attention given to them least Axedents should happen, yet they used the powder Rather too Extravagent, But that was not all They have certainly stolen a Considerable Quantity as we have not more by us that will last until tomorrow noon. Our hole troop is Such Villains that we must for the future give the powder into Charge of a person appointed for that purpose to measure it to them on the ground by a Charger . . . .

Construction of the Great Falls Skirting Canal gave rise to other projects. In 1790 the Virginia legislature granted a charter to Henry Lee for the development of a town on land that he had acquired along the canal. Lee called the settlement Matildaville, after his first wife. It consisted of forty half-acre lots, some of which were purchased by the canal company for construction of a superintendent's residence, offices, a barracks, and houses for clerks and mechanics. Other structures in the vicinity were a few warehouses, a market house, a number of huts and boarding houses, a spring house, an ice house, and Meyers Tavern (later called Dickeys Inn), which survived until 1942. Traces of a few of these structures remain.

Even before completion of the Great Falls Skirting Canal, the Patowmack Company obtained permission in 1798 to collect tolls at Great Falls, provided that the company hauled the cargo around the cataract for no additional charge. Between August 1799 and August 1822, nearly 14,000 craft carrying 164,000 tons of cargo paid tolls to the company. The peak year was 1811, when the company received tolls on 16,350 tons. For the trip from Cumberland to Georgetown, transport costs by water were about half or two-thirds those by land. Boats going downstream carried agricultural products, such as flour, wheat, corn, rye, oats, tobacco, hay, hemp, butter, livestock, and meat. Whiskey poured out of the hinterland. Lumber, furs, and pig iron were also sent to the cities at tidewater. Manufactured goods, tools, and refined products made the return trip.

Most of the traffic, however, was one way: downstream. The ability of the inland settlements to produce substantially exceeded their capacity to consume, and in any case the return trip against the current on the open river was difficult. Long rafts of logs, narrow enough to fit through the locks, carried farm products to market and then were broken up for lumber. Even substantial barges called gondolas were dismantled and sold at journey's end, since such craft were too clumsy to row or push back upriver.

Some craft, however, were designed to make the return trip. One such boat was called the *sharper* because it was pointed at each end. Sharpers resembled oversized canoes, 60 to 75 feet long, 5 to 7 feet wide, and drawing only 1½ feet even when loaded with

20 tons of cargo. Amidships a tarpaulin, like the canvas cover of a Conestoga wagon, was stretched over metal hoops to protect the cargo. A crew of up to three men — required by law to be licensed — guided the boat downriver and laboriously poled it back upstream by pushing against the river bed and walking toward the stern along the boat's running boards. Slightly larger than the sharper was the keelboat, similar in shape but capable of carrying 100 to 125 barrels of flour. For such boats the downstream trip from Cumberland to Georgetown took three to five days, depending on the current, but twelve to eighteen days were required for the return trip.

Navigation on the open river was affected not only by the current but also by annual floods and periods of low water. Despite the charter requirement that the river be made navigable at all seasons, the Patowmack Company never succeeded in clearing a channel for use during summer droughts. The season for river traffic began in February but ceased in May as the river fell and became impassable. Autumn rains brought another brief period when boats could move on the river.

Dissatisfaction with river navigation led to agitation for a continuous canal from tidewater to Cumberland and beyond. At first the Patowmack Company successfully opposed inauguration of the new project, but the company gradually lost influence as its finances became deranged. During the entire period of the corporation's existence, annual expenses always far outstripped revenues, and except for one dividend paid in 1802, shareholders received no return on their investment. The legislatures of Virginia and Maryland constantly pressed the company to clear the Potomac channel and to make other costly improvements. Maryland provided loans to extend navigation up tributaries of the Potomac, but these projects were never finished and did not pay. The company even sponsored a lottery to raise funds but lost money instead. During the War of 1812, traffic on the river declined because of the curtailment of foreign trade. By 1819 the company was insolvent and struggling merely to keep its canals and locks in working order.

In light of the failure of the Patowmack Company, Virginia and Maryland authorized formation of the Chesapeake & Ohio Canal Company in 1824, and in the following year the Patowmack Company agreed to surrender its charter to the new corporation. (See Chapter 13 for a discussion of the C & O Canal.) On August 15, 1828, a few weeks after construction began on the new waterway, the Patowmack Company conveyed its property to the C & O Canal Company and passed into oblivion. As compensation Patowmack creditors and shareholders received C & O stock. At Great Falls the skirting canal was used until 1830, when the lock gates were removed.

AUTOMOBILE: From Exit 13 of the Capital Beltway (I-495) northwest of McLean, take Route 193 (Georgetown Pike) toward Great Falls. Follow Route 193 a little more than 4 miles. At a crossroads marked by a traffic signal, turn right onto Old Dominion Drive. Go about a mile to the park entrance at the end of the road. If you can, park near the visitor center.

WALK: After stopping by the visitor center and viewing Great Falls (and, if you want, walking upstream to see the mouth of the old Patowmack Canal), follow the former canal ditch "downstream" on a wide path several dozen yards back from the edge of the gorge. With the Potomac River toward the left, pass an old mill site near the visitor center.

A gristmill — later converted to a sawmill — was built here in the 1790s; water from the canal was fed through a sluice and carried by a flume to the water wheel. Part of the masonry foundation is still visible. About 120 yards farther down the canal is the site of a forge; the canal ditch seems to vanish at about this point, indicating that the section upstream was maintained as a race for the forge even after the lower section of the canal was abandoned for use by boats.

With the river toward the left, continue on the wide path through a picnic area and into the woods. Fork slightly right to follow the main path through an area that, although now dry, once was a collecting or holding basin above the canal locks.

The left-hand fork just passed follows the top of the retaining wall that held water in the collecting basin. A gap in the wall at the far end is a waste weir, used to drain the basin and canal so that repairs could be made and silt removed.

Turn right across a small bridge at the side of the collecting basin farthest from the Potomac River, then turn left immediately. Pass the remains of a guard gate on the left and the ruins of the Company House uphill in the woods to the right, where Matildaville was located.

The guard gate was located at the lower end of the collecting basin; it was not a lift lock but simply a single set of swing gates that could be closed in case of flood to protect the locks below. The gate posts pivoted in the curved corners of the quoin stones that still are visible.

Continue along the canal ditch to the first lift lock. Bear half-right uphill and along the hillside, then downhill to the second lift lock. With the canal on the left, continue to a level clearing or plateau above the midpoint of a cleft where the canal joined the Potomac River below Great Falls.

The point where the canal turns half-left to head down the cleft was actually within the third lock. The fourth and fifth locks occupied the deep cut. Locks three, four, and five worked in combination, so that the lower gate of the third lock was the upper gate of the fourth, and so on. Flooding has destroyed almost all evidence of the locks themselves, but the location of the gate separating locks four and five can be discerned (when standing in the bottom of the cleft) from three large holes in the wall and a few courses of stone masonry at the top of the rock face on the right.

From the plateau above the midpoint of the deep cut, turn right and follow a footpath marked with blue blazes uphill into the woods. Turn left at a slightly skewed T-intersection. Follow the blue-blazed path to the rim of Mather Gorge. With the river on the left, continue downstream, sometimes near the edge of the gorge and sometimes behind an escarpment of jagged rocks.

Before the Potomac carved Mather Gorge, the trough behind the escarpment was one of the river's channels, as indicated by a few potholes that are visible. (See Chapter 11 for a discussion of the formation of Great Falls and Mather Gorge.)

Eventually, the trail reaches a road. From this point (marked A on the map) you can either continue for a longer walk or turn right along the road for a shorter walk.

For the shorter walk, follow the road away from the river and through a clearing. Join a wide gravel road intersecting from the left. Follow the road back to the visitor center and parking lots.

For the longer walk, cross the road obliquely to the right. Follow the blue-blazed trail down into a small ravine and up the other side. Continue along the edge of a shelf of land above the river. Bear left to pass through a notch in a spine of boulders and along the rocky slope as the blue-blazed trail leads through tangled brush. Continue uphill to a high promentory.

At the top of the slope, follow the blue-blazed path away from the river. Turn left at a T-intersection. With the river downhill to the left, follow a wide path along the top of the ridge, at one point passing a less worn trail that intersects from the right. (This point is marked B on the map.) Eventually, the trail reaches a promentory high above the confluence of Difficult Run and the Potomac River. From here, you can either retrace your steps to point B and from there follow the directions in the last paragraph, or — if you feel able to do a little scrambling — continue more or less straight downhill to Difficult Run and make a loop back to point B.

For the loop, descend steeply on the blue-blazed trail to Difficult Run, where the blue blazes end. After a short side-trip downstream to the Potomac River, follow Difficult Run upstream. Follow the main trail as it detours uphill around a large cascade and along the side of the valley. The path returns to the edge of the stream at a rocky promentory. Continue upstream along the water's edge for 150 yards to another promentory where the earth slope is severely eroded and the rocks project far out into the stream toward a small cascade. Follow a level path along the water's edge about 170 yards past this second promentory, then turn right onto an obscure footpath at the mouth of a large ravine. Follow the path uphill. Turn left at a T-intersection (point B on the map).

From point B on the map, follow the wide path along the top of the ridge, with the Potomac River downhill to the right. Continue straight where the blue-blazed trail by which you came intersects from the right. Eventually, merge with a wide, well-graded gravel road (the carriage road) and follow it right. Pass a dirt road *intersecting from the right. Follow the carriage road through the forest (the swampy woods to the left occupy a former channel of the Potomac River) and back to the visitor center and parking lots.*

10

RIVERBEND PARK

Walking or ski touring — 5 miles (8 kilometers). A footpath extends for several miles along the Virginia shore of the Potomac River above Great Falls. Other trails explore the bordering upland. Dogs must be leashed. The park is open daily, except Christmas, 7 A.M. until sunset. The Riverbend Nature Center is open weekdays, except Tuesday, 9 A.M. to 5 P.M., weekends 2 P.M. to 5 P.M.; closed Thanksgiving, Christmas, and New Year's Day. Managed by the Fairfax County Park Authority (703) 941-5000; nature center (703) 759-3211; visitor center (703) 759-9018.

RIVERBEND PARK typifies the Piedmont landscape along the Potomac River above Great Falls. The Piedmont Plateau, of course, is one of several physiographic provinces, including the Coastal Plain to the east and the Frederick Valley or Leesburg Basin to the west, that follow the trend of the Atlantic coast in bands of varying width. The Potomac flows across the Piedmont from Seneca to Georgetown, crashing over Great Falls about half way inbetween, but as discussed in Chapter 11, the appearance of the valley above Great Falls is quite different from that below.

Above Great Falls, the Potomac River flows within a wide but steep-sided valley. The surrounding countryside remains as rolling upland that slopes abruptly down to the river, at times in high bluffs studded with rocky outcrops. Narrow strips of flood plain form a low, level shelf at the foot of the bluffs, and it is this band of bottomland that is followed along the river by the route described here. The channel is broad and shallow, the current placid. Rock

ledges have been worn down so that they produce occasional riffles and a few mild rapids. There are many islands, but they are merely low mounds or ribbons of sand and gravel deposited by the river itself and are not much higher than the level of floods that occur about once every two years.

The elevated terrain lying immediately adjacent to the river reflects the hardness of the Piedmont bedrock, which includes schist, quartzite, gneiss, serpentine, gabbro, diabase, and other crystalline, metamorphic rocks. These materials are very resistant to erosion. Nonetheless, weathering and chemical decay have produced a thick layer of earthy, rotten rock called *saprolite*, particularly in areas underlain by schist, as is the case at Riverbend Park. Judging from records kept when water wells are drilled, the saprolite lying on the uplands near Riverbend Park is 60 to 80 feet thick, and in places extends to depths of 120 feet. This thick, soft mantle has been shaped into a landscape of rounded hills and broad, shallow valleys by many small streams. Slopes are gentle, as would be expected in easily eroded material. But where larger rivers penetrate to the unweathered bedrock below, valley walls retain a steep profile, as is usual in solid material. The result is a two-tiered landscape, in which the gently rolling, rockless terrain characteristic of the soft saprolite remains as an uneven plateau above precipitous valleys cut into the hard bedrock by large streams and rivers.

As the region's largest river, the Potomac presents the fullest development of this picture. At Riverbend Park the Potomac has carved a valley about two hundred feet lower than the land along Riverbend Road immediately west of the park, and as much as three hundred feet lower than the land four miles to the west. Generally speaking, the bluffs at first rise steeply from the flood plain, reflecting bedrock at or near the surface. But the upper slopes become more gentle as the bedrock grades into saprolite. This valley profile is easily seen along most of the riverside trail described below, as well as along the C & O Canal on the Maryland side of the river.

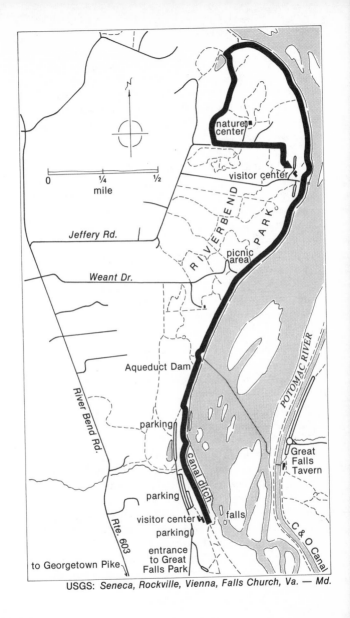

nature center

visitor center

R
I
V
E
R
B
E
N
D

P
A
R
K

Jeffery Rd.

Weant Dr.

picnic area

N

0   ¼   ½
mile

Aqueduct Dam

River Bend Rd.

parking

POTOMAC RIVER

Canal ditch

parking

Great Falls Tavern

visitor center

falls

parking

C & O Canal

Rte. 603

entrance to Great Falls Park

to Georgetown Pike

USGS: *Seneca, Rockville, Vienna, Falls Church, Va. — Md.*

AUTOMOBILE: *The walk described below starts at Great Falls Park, and from there follows the shore upstream to Riverbend Park. Accordingly, from Exit 13 of the Capital Beltway (I-495) northwest of McLean, take Route 193 (Georgetown Pike) toward Great Falls. Follow Route 193 a little more than 4 miles. At a crossroads marked by a traffic signal, turn right onto Old Dominion Drive. Go about a mile to the entrance to Great Falls Park. If you can, park near the visitor center.*

If you want to go directly to Riverbend Park by automobile, continue 0.3 mile north on Route 193 past the crossroads with Old Dominion Drive, then turn right onto Route 603 (River Bend Road). After 2.2 miles, turn right onto Jeffery Road. Follow Jeffery Road almost 1 mile to the entrance to Riverbend Park on the right. Use the map to pick up the route described below or to devise your own. Vehicles not registered in Fairfax County are charged a fee to enter Riverbend Park, except during winter.

WALK: *After viewing Great Falls, head upstream on the old towpath of the Patowmack Canal where it leads past the visitor center. (See Chapter 9 for a discussion of the Patowmack Company and the Great Falls Skirting Canal.) With the canal ditch on your right, follow the path to the head of the former canal at the Potomac River.*

Continue upstream along the shore and then behind a long, skinny island. Eventually, merge with a gravel and dirt road on the left. Follow the gravel and dirt road upstream toward the Aqueduct Dam, from which water for Washington enters the conduit at the Maryland end of the dam. Pass the end of the dam on a footpath, then continue upstream along the shore. Pass through a picnic grove and continue along the flood plain next to the river. Pass another picnic area, a visitor center, and a boat ramp at Riverbend Park. Continue upstream along the shore, at one point passing a trail intersecting from the left.

Eventually, the trail turns into a gravel lane. Follow the gravel lane as it curves left away from the river. Turn left at a T-intersection in front of a pond. Follow a gravel road uphill and through the woods to a hardtop road (Jeffery Road), at one point passing a trail junction where a footpath leads left to the Riverbend Nature Center.

Follow Jeffery Road left. (Walk on the left-hand shoulder to minimize the risk of being hit from behind.) At an intersection where the entrance road to the nature center leads left, continue straight through the woods, passing more roads intersecting from left and right. Follow the road as it bends right, then left downhill to a parking lot behind the visitor center. Continue to the water's edge, then turn right onto the riverside trail. Return downstream to Great Falls by the way you came.

11

GREAT FALLS PARK, MARYLAND
Billy Goat Trail

Walking — 4 miles (6.4 kilometers). Rough going, but well worthwhile. Reached via a short walk along the C & O Canal towpath, the aptly-named Billy Goat Trail crosses rugged terrain along the rim of Mather Gorge. Return past Widewater on the canal towpath. For those who want a less strenuous outing, the towpath provides easy walking to Cropley, where the Berma Road (a dirt and gravel track closed to motor vehicles) leads back toward Great Falls. Dogs must be leashed. The park, which actually is a section of the larger C & O Canal National Historical Park, is open daily from dawn until dusk. The museum at Great Falls Tavern is open daily 9 A.M. to 5 P.M. (or later during summer). Managed by the National Park Service. Great Falls Tavern office (301) 299-3613.

OVERLOOKING THE PRECIPITOUS GORGE of the Potomac River below Great Falls is a bedrock terrace riddled with potholes of the kind that every hiker has seen along rugged riverbeds at low water. Such potholes, of course, are worn by cobbles that are swirled in eddies at the bottom of the river, but at the Potomac gorge the holes are more than sixty feet above the water. The conclusion is clear, even to non-geologists, that the elevated terrace was once part of the riverbed. Other conspicuous features also provide traces of earlier, higher channels, before massive stream erosion created the cataract and gorge we see today.

In broad outline, there is a natural sequence — both in time and place — by which a river dissects an elevated landscape and slowly reduces it to a low plain. At the farthest reaches of the watershed, stormwater runoff carves gullies and steep-sided ravines across the upland. As the streams merge to form a substantial watercourse, the river carves a deeper, wider valley, so that the valley floor is occupied not just by the river itself but also by a flood plain of varying width. Joined by still other tributaries, the river eventually reaches the ocean, which marks a base level and limit for downward stream erosion. But even where downward erosion has ceased, sideward erosion continues as the current is deflected by each curve in the channel. Gradually the river carves a wide valley across which it twists and meanders in an ever-changing course, reducing the surrounding landscape to the level of the river. Meanwhile, the countless gullies and ravines at the river's headwaters continue to fan outward like the roots of a growing tree, so that the watershed becomes bigger and bigger, perhaps even intercepting and diverting to itself streams that previously took a different course to the sea.

Such, at any rate, is the general model. But the actual appearance of any particular stretch of river and the surrounding countryside is determined largely by the durability and structure of the underlying rocks. For example, the Monocacy River, which flows through the Frederick Valley and joins the Potomac River twenty-eight miles upstream from Great Falls, is underlain by soft red sandstone, siltstone, shale, and limestone, all of which are sedimentary rocks that are not particularly resistant to erosion. Consequently, the terrain there has been smoothed into a gently undulating surface by the erosive power of the Monocacy and its tributaries. Flowing past the confluence with the Monocacy, the Potomac occupies a wide, shallow channel bordered by low, wide terraces.

Farther downstream, however, between Seneca and Washington, the Potomac crosses a region of crystalline, metamorphic rock that forms the Piedmont Plateau. The Piedmont materials are more resistant to erosion than the sedimentary rocks farther upstream.

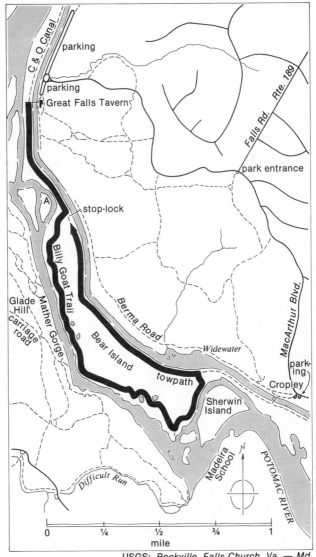

parking

C & O Canal

parking
Great Falls Tavern

Falls Rd. Rte. 189

park entrance

A

stop-lock

Billy Goat Trail

Berma Road

Glade
Hill
carriage
road

Mather Gorge

Bear Island

Widewater

MacArthur Blvd.

parking
Cropley

towpath

Sherwin
Island

Difficult Run

Madeira
School

N

POTOMAC RIVER

| 0 | ¼ | ½ | ¾ | 1 |

mile

USGS: *Rockville, Falls Church, Va. — Md.*

Focusing on the Piedmont region above Great Falls, the Potomac has carved a wide channel disturbed only by minor rapids and riffles, but the resistant Piedmont bedrock remains as a rolling upland sloping abruptly down to the river in high bluffs along each bank. At the foot of the bluffs narrow strips of flood plain border the river.

At Great Falls the picture again changes. There the river encounters a particularly resistant band of rock called *metagraywacke* (pronounced with a long *e* at the end). It is a form of metamorphosed muddy sandstone, somewhat like gneiss, and shows a sugary texture on weathered surfaces. Occurring in a series of vertically tilted strata, some a yard thick, the metagraywacke layers form a barrier that retards erosion above the falls. In effect, these rocks constitute a temporary base level below which the river upstream cannot carve until the barrier is worn away.

Downstream, however, erosion has continued unimpeded. In the vicinity of the river, the Piedmont rocks (primarily mica shist) are hard, but not as resistant as the metagraywacke. While the valley above Great Falls has remained essentially unmodified for about two million years, except for a gradual increase in width, the river below the falls has carved a deep, narrow gorge.

Surviving from the period before the gorge was cut, various features below Great Falls indicate that the river here used to resemble the wider valley seen today immediately above the falls — at Riverbend Park, for example (see Chapter 10). Remnants of the old flood plain and river bottom still stand as terraces perched above the gorge. MacArthur Boulevard follows one of these terraces downstream from Cropley to Cabin John. The C & O Canal occupies the northward extension of this terrace. Another terrace on the Virginia side of the river defines the opposing edge of the former flood plain. In many places these flats are now the rim of the gorge. The terraces occupy a plane which, if projected upstream, still corresponds to the level of the valley floor above Great Falls. Even the islands below Great Falls have flat tops, representing what once was bottomland and river bed. As noted at the outset, in places the terraces are riddled with potholes. Deposits of sand and gravel also indicate that the river once flowed over these areas, although in some cases the deposits are the result of extraordinary floods that have occurred once or twice each century.

Based on this and other evidence, the development of the present landscape can be explained. It appears that about two million years ago, when the level of the ocean was higher than at present, the Potomac had carved a broad channel through the Piedmont upland. At the site of Great Falls, outcrops of metagraywacke caused rapids and split the river into several channels. But with the coming of the Ice Age — or Pleistocene Epoch — sea level fell as water was amassed in continental ice sheets. (Even today, the Ice Age continues at higher latitudes, where enough ice remains to raise the ocean 130 feet if the ice were to melt.) The drop in sea level caused a renewal (or *rejuvenation,* as geologists say) of downward erosion in the broad valley of the Potomac, creating the present-day gorge that extends upstream to the resistant metagraywacke barrier at Great Falls.

To some extent, formation of the gorge below Great Falls was affected by weaknesses in the rock structure. A zone of closely-spaced fractures and joints just below the falls has caused the river to cut laterally toward the Maryland shore and to split into three channels. (From a spectacular vantage point opposite the island marked A on the map, the towpath of the C & O Canal overlooks the two eastern channels, which are dry at low water.) Similarly, the straight chasm called Mather Gorge marks a fault line where erosion along the zone of fracture has been relatively rapid. The existence of the fault is indicated by vertical veins of rock called *dikes,* running more or less at right angles to the gorge; these dikes were intruded into the surrounding bedrock before the fault occurred and so should align if extended across the gorge, but in fact they have been offset more than twenty-five yards by horizontal movement of the opposing faces of the fault.

As the crushed and broken rock along the fault became the site of relatively rapid downward erosion, old channels were left high and dry — or if not dry, as mere sloughs and swamps. One of these

abandoned channels is Widewater, now artificially flooded and incorporated into the C & O Canal (see the map). Another is the swamp behind Glade Hill on the Virginia shore, next to the carriage road.

The result is the river that we see today, but, of course, it is by no means the final result. Erosion continues, and eventually the barrier of resistant metagraywacke at Great Falls will be worn away and breached, so that downward cutting will advance upstream into the valley above the falls, producing a chasm like the one farther downstream. Erosion below the falls will continue to deepen the gorge until the river approaches sea level (now reached at Washington). Even after the river digs down to zero elevation, sideward cutting will continue to widen the valley. Or, as some people speculate, large sections of polar ice may melt, causing the sea to flood the gorge, as already has occurred in the "drowned" valleys of Chesapeake Bay and its various tidal rivers. Check back in another two million years.

AUTOMOBILE: From the Capital Beltway (I-495) west of Washington, take Exit 41 for Carderock. (This exit is further identified by being the first north of the Potomac River or the first south of the interchange with Cabin John Parkway.) Follow the Maryland branch of the George Washington Memorial Parkway west past the exit for Carderock Recreation Area and the Naval Ship Research and Development Center. Turn left at a T-intersection with MacArthur Boulevard. Follow MacArthur Boulevard west 2.2 miles to an intersection with Falls Road at the entrance to Great Falls Park. Continue straight into the park and downhill along the winding road that leads to the parking lots by the Chesapeake & Ohio Canal.

WALK: Cross the canal on the footbridge at Lock 20 next to Great Falls Tavern. With the canal on the left, head downstream along the towpath. Pass Locks 19,

18, and 17. About 30 yards before a high footbridge over the canal (the bridge is located at a stop-lock and levee to divert floods), turn right onto the Billy Goat Trail, which is marked with blue blazes. (If you suspect that the aptly-named Billy Goat Trail will be too strenuous for you, the map shows that it is possible to continue on the towpath to a causeway below Widewater, then return on the opposite side of the canal to the stop-lock and high bridge.)

Follow the rocky blue-blazed trail through the woods. Bear half-left to follow the blue blazes across rugged terrain at the rim of the gorge. For the most part, the trail lies somewhat back from the edge.

Continue as the blue-blazed trail veers half-right across an area of large, jumbled rocks pitted with potholes, indicating that this area was once part of the riverbed. Continue behind an escarpment of jagged rocks at the edge of the gorge. Eventually, descend toward the river, then climb diagonally along a sloping face of rock. (If you are uncomfortable at the prospect of scrambling up this rocky slope, retrace your steps 50 or 60 yards, then follow a faint trail that detours toward the end of the rocks and up through a cleft; once above the rocks, bushwhack to the right until you rejoin the blue-blazed trail at the rim of the gorge.)

Continue over rocky terrain on the blue-blazed trail, sometimes near the edge of the gorge and sometimes at a distance from the rim. Follow the blue blazes as the trail descends, climbs, and winds over bare rocks and past several ponds and hills. Eventually, the trail reaches a point of rocks above a large channel of the Potomac that is dry during low water. The hill beyond is Sherwin Island; beyond that, on the heights of the opposite shore, is the Madiera School. Follow the blue-blazed trail toward the left. Keeping the large channel on the right, continue across rocky hills and ravines.

The trail joins the canal and towpath at the lower end of Widewater. With the canal on the right, follow the towpath back to the starting point at Great Falls.

12

GREAT FALLS PARK, MARYLAND
Gold Mine Tract

Walking or ski touring — 4.5 miles (7.2 kilometers). Easy hiking along the C & O Canal towpath and the Berma Road (a dirt and gravel track closed to motor vehicles). Continue around the loop on woodland trails that weave, dip, and climb across heights dissected by shallow ravines. A spur trail leads to the ruins of the Maryland Mine, last in a series of gold mines at Great Falls. Dogs must be leashed. The park, which actually is a section of the larger C & O Canal National Historical Park, is open daily from dawn until dusk. The museum at Great Falls Tavern is open daily 9 A.M. to 5 P.M. (or later during summer). Managed by the National Park Service. Great Falls Tavern office (301) 299-3613.

THERE'S GOLD IN THEM THAR HILLS at Great Falls. And not just gold but the trenches, pits, and ruins of abandoned mines, one of which ceased operating as recently as 1940.

Fantasies, rumors, and reports of gold in the Chesapeake region are as old as the first European settlers. In his *Adventures and Discourses,* Captain John Smith mentions how glad he was when a certain Captain Martin left Jamestown to return to England in 1608, for Martin "was always hankering after finding that gold, which did not exist, thereby creating great disunion amongst us . . . ." On another occasion, Smith relates that the colonists who arrived at Jamestown included two refiners and two goldsmiths: "And, again, see how the lust of finding gold, was apparent in their sending out refiners and goldsmiths, who never had occasion to exercise their craft . . . ." Nonetheless, while exploring the Potomac

River, Smith himself showed considerable interest in a place where the sand was "mingled with yellow spangles." He asked Matchqueono, the King of Patawomeke, about the metal, and was conducted by Indian guides to a mine seven or eight miles inland:

> The mine was a great rocky mountain like antimony, in which they had digged a great hole with their shells and hatchets. Hard by ran a fair brook of crystal-like water, in which they washed away the dross and kept the remainder, which they put in little bags and sell all over the country, where it is used to paint their bodies, faces, or their idols; which makes them look like blackamores dusted over with silver . . . .

Smith sent some of the material to England to be assayed. The result was strangely contradictory: he was told later that the dust was half silver but that it "proved of no value." In any case, nothing came of the matter.

The first authentic report of gold in Maryland occurred when traces were found in 1849 on a farm near Brookville in Montgomery County, Maryland, but no production is recorded. A dozen years later, gold was discovered near Great Falls by a Union soldier whose Pennsylvania regiment camped in the area during the autumn and winter after the first battle of Manassas. According to one account, this man was either Private Alexander McCleary or Private John Carey, both of whom are listed on the regimental rolls at that time. By another account, the soldier (whoever he was) found specks of gold while washing skillets in a stream near Cropley. Following his discharge from the army, he supposedly organized a group of investors who bought the farm on which the discovery was made. In any case, prospecting did indeed begin, and in 1867, after considerable investigation, the mining company sank a shaft a hundred feet into a seam of gold-bearing quartz. This shaft was about two hundred feet south of the ruins (still visible today) of the Maryland Mine, an operation that was developed later just downhill from the intersection of Falls Road and MacArthur Boulevard (see the map). Production, however, was disappointing and the work was soon abandoned.

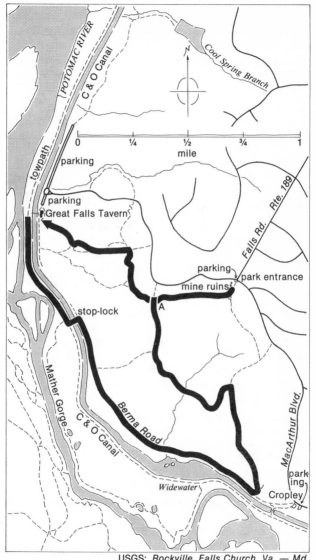

POTOMAC RIVER

C & O Canal

Cool Spring Branch

0   ¼   ½   ¾   1
mile

towpath

parking

parking

Great Falls Tavern

parking

park entrance

mine ruins

Falls Rd. Rte. 189

stop-lock

A

Mather Gorge

C & O Canal

Berma Road

MacArthur Blvd.

parking

Cropley

Widewater

USGS: *Rockville, Falls Church, Va. — Md.*

In the 1880s a prospector from Georgia found gold about a mile to the north of the earlier mine. By 1890 large pits had been dug in the side of the ravine at Cool Spring Branch, which joins the Potomac about nine hundred yards north of the Great Falls parking lot. A small processing mill operated near the mouth of the stream.

During the following three decades, considerable prospecting and mining were done in the area between Cool Spring Branch and the site of the Maryland Mine. More shafts were sunk in the uplands, and more pits and tunnels were dug in the sides of ravines by a series of companies, including the Great Falls Gold Mining Co., the Maryland Gold Mining Co., and the Empress Gold Mining Co., each trying to succeed where its predecessors and rivals failed. In May 1901, the *Maryland Journal* reported six gold mines in operation along the Potomac River upstream from Washington. The most systematic effort was made by the Atlantic Development Company, which during World War I undertook extensive trenching, stripping, and drilling on more than 2,100 acres that it had acquired in the Great Falls area. A series of long trenches stretching east and west are still discernible in aerial photographs as parallel lines running through woods and fields and up and down hills and ravines. Some of the side trails shown on the map cross these trenches. In 1917 surface exploration was abandoned and the mines were closed, but the next year the Maryland Mine was reopened, worked for three years, then closed again.

Gold fever, however, was not long in remission. In 1934 the price of gold rose to $35 an ounce, and the next year the Maryland Mining Company was organized. The Maryland Mine was opened again and a new mill was installed for crushing the quartz into fine ore. A photograph of the mill shows a heavy timber contraption resembling a series of sheds and shanties built on stilts and stuck together at different levels. From the mill, the ore passed through an amalgamator, where the gold particles were chemically extracted by amalgamation with mercury. Later the amalgam was processed to yield pure gold and to recycle the mercury.

In its new (and so far, last) incarnation, the Maryland Mine processed about 6,000 tons of ore, yielding 2,570 ounces of gold worth nearly $800,000 at January 1985 prices. The mine closed in 1940, but since then prospecting has continued, as has panning for gold in local streams, especially after surges in the price of gold. To pan for gold on Federal property at Great Falls, permission must first be obtained from the park superintendent.

The mining activities at Great Falls have revealed that the principal vein of gold-bearing quartz occurs as a seam that meets the surface in a curved line extending about two miles from the mouth of Cool Spring Branch in the north to the eastern end of Widewater in the south (as the bulge in the C & O Canal is called). Other scattered seams run more or less parallel with the main vein. The gold occurs as grains, wires, or sheets in the quartz, which in turn occupies fault zones in the surrounding metamorphic rocks. The distribution of gold in the seams is erratic, and this lack of consistency has been one of the chief obstacles to large-scale development of the deposits, most of which have only marginal gold content. Nonetheless, a few rich pockets have been found. Of the gold recovered from the Maryland Mine between 1936 and 1940, more than 8 percent came from only 70 pounds of ore, or that is, from .0006 percent of the 6,000 tons of ore that were processed.

A word of caution: The old mine shafts and tunnels have not been maintained. They are extremely dangerous and should not be entered.

AUTOMOBILE: From the Capital Beltway (I-495) west of Washington, take Exit 41 for Carderock. (This exit is further identified by being the first north of the Potomac River or the first south of the interchange with Cabin John Parkway.) Follow the Maryland branch of the George Washington Memorial Parkway west past the exit for Carderock Recreation Area and the Naval Ship Research and Development Center. Turn left at a T-intersection with MacArthur Boulevard. Follow

MacArthur Boulevard west 2.2 miles to an intersection with Falls Road at the entrance to Great Falls Park. Continue straight into the park and downhill along the winding road that leads to the parking lots by the Chesapeake & Ohio Canal.

WALK: Cross the canal on the footbridge at Lock 20 next to Great Falls Tavern. With the canal on the left, head downstream along the towpath. Pass Locks 19, 18, and 17. Continue to a high footbridge over the canal at a stop-lock and levee designed to divert floods. Cross the high bridge over the canal, then turn right onto a gravel road, called by punsters the Berma Road, because it follows what in canal jargon is termed the berm — i.e., the bank opposite the towpath. The Berma Road lies atop the Washington Aqueduct, which carries water from the Potomac River at Great Falls to the capital.

With the canal on the right, follow the Berma Road more than a mile, passing at the outset Lock 16 and a lockkeeper's house. For a period the road and canal are separated by woods, but south of Widewater, the road again overlooks the canal. Eventually, where the road passes to the right of a chainlink enclosure, veer left onto an obscure footpath marked with green blazes. Follow the green-blazed footpath behind the chainlink enclosure, then sharply left uphill. Continue as the path gradually becomes wider and follows an old roadbed through the woods.

At one point the trail follows a raised, dike-like roadbed for 30 yards across the head of a ravine. About 50 yards beyond the end of the raised roadbed, turn left onto a blue-blazed trail. (Both green and blue blazes mark the trail that continues straight.)

After turning left onto the blue-blazed trail, continue through the woods, then gradually downhill to the right and along the side of a shallow ravine. Cross the bottom of a larger ravine and continue uphill. Eventually, about 100 yards after crossing the top of the hill, pass a yellow-blazed trail intersecting from the left. Continue straight ahead on the path marked with both blue and yellow blazes. After about 350 yards, reach a trail intersection (marked A on the map) where the yellow-blazed trail continues straight and footpaths marked with blue blazes lead left and right. If you reach a paved road — the park entrance road — you have missed the trail junction and should retrace your steps 170 yards.

From the trail junction at point A, the right-hand footpath leads east about two-fifths of a mile toward the wreckage of the Maryland Mine, located just below the intersection of Falls Road and MacArthur Boulevard. If you want to walk to the mine ruins, follow the trail 400 yards, for the most part parallel with an old prospecting trench on the left. At a pit next to the trench, continue downhill another 140 yards, then turn left uphill; climb 100 yards to the wreckage of the mine; the main shafts are another 100 yards uphill. Do not attempt to enter the shafts, which are dangerous. The mine ruins can also be seen as you leave the park at the end of your excursion; park in the informal lot at the intersection of Falls Road and MacArthur Boulevard, then walk into the woods 60 yards. There are more mine ruins farther downhill.

To continue on the main circuit from point A, follow the blue-blazed footpath west (i.e., left, as viewed from your original approach to the trail junction). Follow the trail as it winds gradually downhill, passing the mounds of Allegheny mound-building ants. Fork right to continue on the blue-blazed path as it zigzags through the woods. Eventually, at a four-way intersection, turn left onto the former trolley roadbed of the Washington & Great Falls Railway.

Follow the wide path through a cut and then along a section of raised roadbed. Where the embankment splits into a Y, fork right. (The embankment forms a loop that used to be a turn-around at the end of the trolley line.) At the farthest point of the loop — i.e., about 115 yards from the fork in the trail — turn right and descend from the embankment. Fork right again and follow the blue-blazed footpath downhill along the side of a ravine on the right. Continue as the ravine narrows shortly before reaching the canal near Great Falls Tavern. Turn right to return to the parking lot.

13

CHESAPEAKE & OHIO CANAL
Violets Lock to Georgetown

*Walking, bicycling, or ski touring — up to 22 miles, one way
(35.4 kilometers). The broad, level towpath of the C & O
Canal follows the Potomac River, linking countryside and city
and providing a walkway unsurpassed on the East Coast for
scenery and historical interest. Hike from Violets Lock to
Georgetown (or vice versa) along the entire section of canal
that still holds water and retains the appearance of a working
canal. Although the walking is easy, only enthusiasts will
want to cover the entire distance in one day. Several access
points at intervals of five to seven miles are described under
the automobile directions, making possible a series of shorter
trips. If you do not want to retrace your steps, a car shuttle is
necessary. Dogs must be leashed. Managed by the National
Park Service. Great Falls Tavern office (301) 299-3613.*

THE TOWPATH of the Chesapeake & Ohio Canal extends 185
miles along the Maryland bank of the Potomac River between
Cumberland and Georgetown. Most of the canal itself is empty and
overgrown, but for the twenty-two miles nearest Georgetown, the
canal has been restored to its appearance during the first quarter of
the twentieth century, when it was still an operating commercial
waterway. Lift locks and lockkeepers' houses, stop gates and levees
to divert floods, feeder canals to bring in water and spillways to
drain off the excess, aqueducts to carry the entire canal across
tributaries of the Potomac, and other intriguing engineering works
punctuate a walk along the towpath.

The continuous canal along the Maryland shore was the successor to a project of the Patowmack Company, which between 1785 and 1802 built five short canals that skirted the river's worst falls and rapids. Although the Potomac River was thus made navigable between Cumberland and Georgetown, the system worked only during periods of high water. By 1819 the Patowmack Company was bankrupt, and in 1828 it conveyed all its rights and property along the river to the newly-formed Chesapeake & Ohio Canal Company. At Little Falls just west of Georgetown, the C & O Canal was built atop the Patowmack Company's old skirting canal. (For a discussion of the Patowmack Company, see Chapter 9.)

The practicality of a continuous, man-made waterway to the West was demonstrated in 1825 by the completion of the Erie Canal connecting Buffalo and Albany. By linking the Great Lakes with the Hudson River, the Erie project provided cheap transport for heavy loads between what was then called the Northwest (and is now termed the Middle West) and New York City. Alarmed that the potentially vast trade with the interior of the country would be channeled through New York, other Eastern cities and states began building their own canals.

On July 4, 1828 — the same day that construction began on the Baltimore & Ohio Railroad, the nation's first commercial rail venture — President John Quincy Adams broke ground for the C & O Canal. The waterway was to extend 360 miles to the Ohio River at Pittsburgh. The Federal government and the city of Washington each subscribed for $1,000,000 in stock; Maryland put up $500,000, Georgetown and Alexandria each contributed $250,000, Shepherdstown $2,000, and individuals $607,400. But by 1850, when the canal reached Cumberland, costs had mounted to almost three times the original estimate for construction of the entire canal, and many millions of dollars had been paid in interest during a period when the waterway produced only negligible income. Maryland had paid an additional $5,000,000 toward the project, jeopardizing the state's credit; other investors simply refused to advance additional funds. In the meantime the

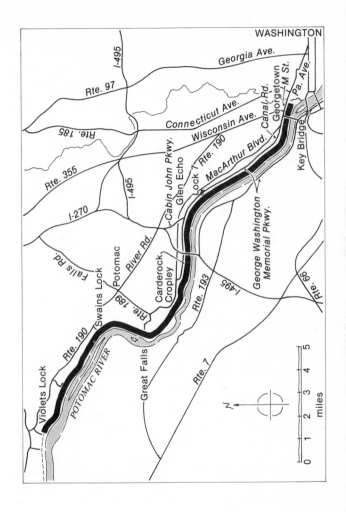

Baltimore & Ohio Railroad had reached Cumberland in 1842 and had forged westward across the Allegheny Mountains. By 1852 the railroad stretched to the Ohio River at Wheeling, and plans to extend the canal beyond Cumberland were abandoned.

The slow pace and high cost of construction reflected a series of logistical, legal, and labor problems. Building stone, lumber, and lime for cement were chronically in short supply. Excavation often revealed unexpected rock, hardpan, or other difficult materials close to the surface. West of Point of Rocks, where the B & O Railroad also follows the Potomac Valley, competition for a right-of-way led to high land prices, litigation, and delay. Because of the shortage of manpower in America, laborers, stone cutters, masons, carpenters, and even miners were brought from England, Wales, the Netherlands, Germany, and Ireland, often on an indentured basis. Brawls occurred between antagonistic Irish factions, and more than a few men were beaten to death in pitched battles, culminating in January 1834, when Federal troops were summoned to restore order. The episode ended with a formal treaty signed by twenty-eight leaders of the warring groups, but labor unrest flared again at different camps and among different groups as construction dragged on. Dissatisfied with poor food, makeshift barracks and shacks, low and often tardy pay, and indentured servitude, many workers simply ran away, and still others died in epidemics that swept through the labor camps.

Even after the canal was finished as far as Cumberland, its upkeep and improvement demanded large expenditures. Floods frequently damaged the waterway and locks, and the Civil War brought further destruction that required extensive repairs. Because of Maryland's huge financial commitment to the canal, the waterway became, in effect, a government operation; the corporation's officers were appointed by the state and preference for low-level jobs, such as lock tending, was given to Civil War veterans.

The canal's most prosperous period was the 1870s, when more than seven hundred mule-drawn boats were in operation. Eastbound cargo consisted mainly of grain, building stone, lumber, whiskey, and above all else, coal from Cumberland. Westbound boats carried miscellaneous provisions and manufactured goods, but the tonnage going upstream was always much less than that going down.

But even during the canal's peak years, profits did little more than pay the interest on the enormous construction debt, which, in fact, was never repaid. After a disastrous flood in 1889 left the waterway in ruin, the canal company incurred still more debt to rebuild. During the first two decades of the twentieth century, tonnage carried by the canal gradually declined as the Baltimore & Ohio Railroad acquired control of the waterway by purchasing the canal company's shares and bonds. When a flood in April 1924 tore long gaps in the canal bank, the waterway was abandoned. By then 87 percent of the canal company's shares were owned by the rival B & O, which had long since demonstrated the superior flexibility and efficiency of the railways. But the B & O in turn became financially troubled during the Great Depression, and in 1938, at the suggestion of Secretary of the Interior Harold Ickes, the railroad conveyed the canal to the Federal government in satisfaction of an unpaid debt of $2 million owed the Reconstruction Finance Corporation, a Depression-era agency that made loans to hard-pressed industries. For a period the Department of the Interior considered using the canal right-of-way for an automobile parkway, but eventually preservationists prevailed, and administrative and legislative action taken in 1961 and 1971 established the C & O Canal National Historical Park, combining outstanding scenery and a fascinating glimpse of the past.

An excellent description of life on the Chesapeake & Ohio Canal in 1859 is provided by a manuscript of an unknown author who, as the guest and helper of a boat captain, made the trip from Cumberland to Georgetown, across the Potomac to Alexandria via the Alexandria Aqueduct and Canal, then back to Cumberland. Aside from the author and the captain, the crew consisted of a Negro bow man named Pic and two boys who took turns guiding a team of mules along the towpath. There were four mules, and the usual routine was to work them in shifts of two. Loaded with 120 tons of coal and moving at a steady pace of about two miles per hour, the boat had great momentum, and this made passing through the locks an operation that required considerable skill:

> To enter a lock requires care and experience. The boat had to be steered in a direct line in the center of the canal, for the least deviation would cause a collision with the stone walls that might sink it, for it fitted the lock like a nickle in a slot. The boat must also have sufficient motion to carry it to the end of the lock and at the same time it must not strike the lower gate. The Capt. steered the boat in, Pic stood on the bow and jumped ashore with a line and give it two turns around the snubbing post. At the right moment the Capt. gave the word to the tow boy to stop; Pic tightened the rope on the post and the boat came to a standstill just before the cutwater touched the gate. The friction of the rope around the post has to be carefully governed or the momentum of the boat and its load will break it. This friction and the rubbing of the boat against the side of the lock and the force of the water confined in the end of the lock combined to bring the boat to a stop.

After a boat heading down the canal had floated into the lock, the upstream gates were closed and sluices in the downstream gates were opened, lowering the water to the level of the canal below the lock. Then the downstream gates were opened and the boat towed out. For boats headed up the canal, the procedure was reversed; the water in the lock was raised by opening sluices in the upstream gates after the boat was sealed in the lock. Alerted by the blast of a trumpet carried on each boat, the lockkeeper would have the water at the right level and the appropriate gates open for an approaching boat, whose crew would help operate the sluices and the gates as the boat passed through the lock.

In order to maximize capacity, most boats were made to fit the locks closely, with the result that the standard craft was 90 feet long, 14½ feet wide, and drew 4½ feet when fully loaded. At each end was a cabin with the roof raised about three feet above the deck. The forward cabin was a stable where the mules rode and rested when they were not in harness. The aft cabin held a galley and a couple of berths. Between the cabins was the hold, covered with hatches, and amidships was a small cabin-like structure holding feed and hay for the mules. Behind the aft cabin was a small tiller deck. According to the anonymous account mentioned before, "A hundred or more of these boats were brought from the Erie canal, when that was enlarged, by the canal companies who now own nearly all the boats, the boatmen furnishing teams and outfit, receiving so much a ton for hauling the coal, paying their own expenses and the toll on the empty boat back to Cumberland."

The days were long and monotonous:

We were tied up to no regular hours and lived in Arcadian simplicity. We rose with the early morning light, fed the mules, and when they had eaten their breakfast a pair was hitched up and we started on our day's journey driving them about four hours when they were changed for the other pair; at the end of the next four hours they were again changed, and so on making four shifts and sailing from sixteen to eighteen hours a day, the Capt., Pic and myself taking turns at the rudder while the two boys changed off from time to time and occasionally Pic and myself would drive for an hour or two, walking for exercise; the boys usually rode the rear mule.

Some days the four mules were hitched tandem, then we drove about twelve hours, with a short rest at noon, ungearing them to let them roll which seemed to refresh them nearly as much as a half day's rest. These might seem long days to work in the present eight and ten hours times, but as far as the work was concerned, it mattered little whether the boat sailed or not. There were the meals to cook, someone must stand at the tiller, and the mules must be driven, and there was about five minutes work for one of the others at each lock, the rest of the time could be spent reading, sleeping, viewing the landscape or telling stories, in which all but the boy driving could take part . . . .

Along the canal at villages, or important agricultural districts, or where valleys break through the mountains, there were warehouses where mule feed and other boat stores including bread could be procured, and where goods could be received and delivered by the boats, and occasionally there were basins where several boats could be stored to turn around, for the canal was not wide enough to turn a loaded boat . . . .

Once in a while the boat would take a quantity of hay or grain on speculation and peddle it out to the other boats. We met one who had oats for sale and we bought a few bushels at a discount but found when we used them that they were so light in weight that we had paid more than they were worth. Every boat carries what might be called ship papers, that is a bill of lading which states what you have carried for freight to the smallest item, and the distance it was carried, as the canal charges toll on all freight and also on the boat itself. These papers have to be subscribed to under oath. The only extra freight we had was two barrels of whiskey sent from one village to another. Pic and the Capt. sampled the whiskey by driving down a hoop and boring a small hole with a gimlet and drawing out a flask-full. After plugging the hole they drove the hoop back and none but the crew were the wiser for it. On the previous trip the Capt. had a boat load of timber from some point up the canal to Cumberland . . . .

The first question asked a boatman is how do you live on board. We had a small cook stove in which we burned the soft coal with which the boat was loaded, a spider, an iron teakettle, plates, knives, forks, and several of the small cooking utensils including a molasses jug. The bread was purchased at the warehouses along the canal and at the village grocery stores. Ham and bread was the standby. Luxuries in the shape of fresh meat and vegetables were occasionally purchased.

It was bread, dried bread, bread and molasses, and bread. Ham, fried ham, and ham that made up the usual variety. By bringing the slices of ham to a boil in one or two changes of water removed much of the salt and smoke and made it much more palatable and tender. Potatoes when we had them were boiled in the teakettle, then the coffee was made and the dish water heated all in the same utensil. I did most of the cooking but shall not brag of any fancy dishes for I lacked that essential for young housekeepers, a cook book . . . .

Boating was a profitable business when they had a lucky season. If I remember rightly they had about one dollar a ton for transporting the coal when you used your own boat and somewhat less in the company's boats. With a good team two round trips could be made in each month from April to December and the expense was for the help, board, team, and seven dollars toll on each return trip. It was easy to figure a profit on this basis especially in the dull times and low prices that followed the panic of 1857, but the "ifs" were so many that the margin for profit was very small. Sometimes they had to wait for their load at Cumberland as you had to take your turn with the other boats, or there might be an accident at the mines or on their railroad as they might be filling a special order by rail and there is always the possibility of a strike. Then the delay at the other end of the canal was often longer for a storm or head wind sometimes prevents the arrival of any schooners sometimes for weeks. You might wait in Georgetown or Alexandria for a chance to unload while your neighbor made two round trips for one of the other lines. Still worse than these were the breaks and wash-outs on the canal that detained all the boats alike [;] these sometimes caused months' delay . . . . In some season these breaks will follow one after the other until the whole season is used up and in the fall the boatmen will not have enough money to pay expenses. There was more or less freight to be carried besides the coal but as Washington was not a commercial city a larger share went to and from Baltimore. Sometimes the boatmen and warehousemen would pick up a boat of fruit or grain to be sold on speculation and after harvest there was considerable wheat and corn delivered to the mills at Georgetown but when all the local freight was divided among the three or four hundred boats it amounted to very little to

each. At the end of the season the navigation is closed. It is
desirable to keep the canal open as long as possible and not have
the boats freeze in or the locks freeze up and burst. When
freezing weather grows near a day is appointed giving a few
weeks' notice when the canal will be drawn off, then there is a
hurrying around with their last load and getting their boats home
or in some place where they can lay in safety until spring. There
would of course be a few who would be belated . . . and find
themselves stranded along the canal.

Sometimes on the more northern canals nature will close the
canal before the appointed time catching hundreds of boats in
transit. On the day appointed the . . . gates are closed and the
water drawn off from every canal except the one at Georgetown
which supplies the mills and during the winter the canal is
cleaned and the many needed repairs made. The next spring
soon after the arrival of the bluebird the water is turned in and
as the canal is free from ice the navigation is resumed.

For those who navigated the C & O Canal, boating was a
unique way of life handed down from father to son. During the
declining years of the waterway, few outsiders were drawn to the
work, which paid poorly. "The children are brought up on the boat
and don't know nothin' else, and that is the only reason they take
up boating," one mother told investigators from the Federal
Children's Bureau in 1921. She continued: "Boys work for their
fathers until they are big enough to get a boat of their own, and it's
always easy to get a boat." At the time of the Federal survey, most
C & O captains carried their wives and children with them, with
the result that the children did not attend school for more than a
fraction of the year; few children finished the elementary grades
and many were illiterate.

Aside from doing the cooking, washing, and other "household"
chores, the wives at times helped to steer the boat. Except in critical
circumstances, the children too took turns steering, and also drove
the mules, walking or riding for long hours in all weather. The
boats were kept moving for as much of the day and night as each

family could stand; fifteen hours per day was a minimum, eighteen hours typical, and some boats were operated longer or even continuously. "We don't know it's Sunday," said one captain and father, "til we see some folks along the way, dressed up and a 'goin' to Sunday school." And according to another captain, "The women and children are as good as the men. If it weren't for the children the canal wouldn't run a day."

On the standard C & O Canal boat, the aft cabin, where the family lived, was only ten by twelve feet, with two narrow berths, each used by two people. Often children had to sleep on the floor or the deck or in the feed box where hay was stored for the mules. In pleasant weather, the family spent most of their time on deck, but cooking on a coal stove had to be done in the stifling heat of the cabin. Some families lived in their boats year round, even when the craft sat on the bottom of the canal during winter, but most had small homes at some point along the canal.

Today a corps of canal enthusiasts are as firmly bound to the C & O Canal as the boatmen ever were. One of the chief interpreters of the canal has been Thomas F. Hahn, author or editor of numerous books from which much of the information contained here has been obtained. These works and other canal literature are available from the American Canal and Transportation Center, Box 310, Shepherdstown, WV 25443. For a complete listing of the center's publications, send a self-addressed stamped envelope.

AUTOMOBILE: Several access points, each between 5 and 7 miles apart, are described below.

Violets Lock is near milepost 22 on the canal. From Exit 39 of the Capital Beltway (I-495) northwest of Washington, take Route 190 (River Road) west to the town of Potomac. From the intersection with Route 189 (Falls Road) at the center of Potomac, continue west on Route 190 for 7.8 miles to Violets Lock Road on the left. Follow Violets Lock Road to the parking lot next to the canal.

Swains Lock is about 16.5 miles along the canal from Georgetown. Follow the directions for Violets Lock in the preceding paragraph, but continue only 2.1 miles west of Potomac on Route 190. Turn left onto Swains Lock Road and follow it to the canal.

Cropley is near milepost 12 on the canal. From the Capital Beltway west of Washington, take Exit 41 for Carderock. (This exit is further identified by being the first north of the Potomac River or the first south of the interchange with Cabin John Parkway.) Follow the Maryland branch of the George Washington Memorial Parkway west past the exit for Carderock Recreation Area and the Naval Ship Research and Development Center. Turn left at a T-intersection with MacArthur Boulevard. Follow MacArthur Boulevard west 1.1 miles to the parking lot opposite Old Angler's Inn. Join the towpath by walking downhill on the dirt road.

Lock 7 is at milepost 7 on the canal. If you are traveling clockwise — i.e., from Virginia to Maryland — on the Capital Beltway, exit for Glen Echo immediately after crossing the Potomac River; follow the Maryland branch of the George Washington Memorial Parkway toward Glen Echo and Washington 2.0 miles to the C & O Canal Lock 7 parking area on the right. If you are traveling counter-clockwise on the Capital Beltway, take Exit 40 for Cabin John Parkway; after merging with the George Washington Memorial Parkway, go 0.5 mile to the Lock 7 parking area on the right. If you are approaching from Georgetown via Canal Road and the parkway, go to the exit labeled Cabin John (taking care not to exit earlier for MacArthur Boulevard or I-495 North); at the Cabin John exit, make a U-turn over the parkway, then return 0.8 mile to the Lock 7 parking area. Finally, from the Lock 7 parking lot, there is no direct access to the westbound lanes of the parkway, so to return to I-495, drive east a few hundred yards to the first exit on the left; bear very sharply left, then left again immediately to reach the parkway westbound.

Georgetown, of course, is at the canal terminus. In Georgetown the canal runs parallel with M Street, from which the towpath can be reached by walking downhill on almost any cross street. Georgetown can be reached by automobile from the north via Route 355, which is served by Exit 34 for Bethesda off the Capital Beltway; Route 355 becomes Wisconsin Avenue, which leads to M Street in the center of Georgetown. From the east, M Street and Georgetown can be reached via Pennsylvania Avenue. From the south, the Key Bridge leads to M Street in Georgetown. And from the west, follow the directions for Lock 7 in the preceding paragraph, but continue on the Maryland branch of the George Washington Memorial Parkway as it turns into Canal Road and then into M Street.

WALK: It is possible, of course, to follow the canal towpath either upstream or down. The latter has the advantage of ending at Georgetown, where there are numerous eateries and watering holes for those who want to celebrate the completion of the trip. As the historic terminus for most cargo carried on the canal, Georgetown provides a strong sense of destination, as well as an interesting place to wait if you need to be met by someone with a car. In any case, walking directions are provided to get you started in either direction.

Starting at Violets Lock, cross a bridge over the canal, then a second bridge over a feeder canal. With the canal on the left, follow the towpath downstream 22 miles to Georgetown. As you approach Georgetown, the path crosses from the right bank to the left on the first footbridge downstream from the Key Bridge. (The footbridge slopes slightly toward the river; it is near a row of townhouses with two sculptured horseheads mounted on the end wall.) Continue downstream through Georgetown to Lock 1 next to the Rock Creek and Potomac Parkway.

Starting at Georgetown, pick up the canal on the west side of the Rock Creek and Potomac Parkway just south of the Pennsylvania Avenue bridge over Rock Creek. With the canal on the left, follow the brick path through Georgetown. Pass a series of refurbished mill buildings and go under several automobile and pedestrian bridges. After passing under a small pedestrian truss bridge that slopes slightly toward the left, turn right and double back uphill on a ramp in order to cross the canal on the pedestrian bridge. With the canal on the right, follow the towpath 22 miles upstream to Violets Lock.

14

SENECA CREEK STATE PARK

Walking — 4 miles (6.4 kilometers). Follow interconnected trails along Great Seneca Creek, Long Draught Branch, and the shore of Clopper Lake. Farmed for two centuries, most of the area now has reverted to woods, but extensive meadows are maintained in the vicinity of the lake. Dogs are prohibited. The park is open daily; from April through September, it opens at 8 A.M.; from October through March, it opens at 10 A.M.; at all times of the year, the park closes at sunset. Managed by the Maryland Forest, Park, and Wildlife Service (301) 924-2127. Telephone for information about canoe and sailboat rental and other boating opportunities at Clopper Lake.

SENECA CREEK STATE PARK, which comprises about six thousand acres in all, extends from the vicinity of Gaithersburg downstream thirteen miles to the Potomac River, but only the northern section around Clopper Lake is developed for walking and other activities. Clopper Lake itself is a recent creation, made by damming Long Draught Branch, but the name "Clopper" goes back in this neighborhood to the early nineteenth century, when Francis C. Clopper acquired the land. The tract remained in the ownership of his descendants through four generations until purchased by the state in 1955. Starting at the site of the former Clopper house, the walk described here follows streams that used to supply water power to Clopper's various mills, and crosses woods and fields that previously were part of the large Clopper farm.

One enterprise was Clopper Mill, which actually predates the period of Clopper ownership. According to a patent, or deed, dating from 1777, when Montgomery County was only sparsely settled, Nicholas Sybert, "yeoman," conveyed to Benjamin Spyker, also styled yeoman, 222 acres of land "with all and singular the improvements, mills, ways, water and watercourses" on Great Seneca Creek at what is now the present mill site. Sybert had patented the land nine years earlier, and apparently it was he who first built a mill there.

By 1783 the property was owned by William Benson, who contracted to sell the tract "Good Part" to Zachariah Maccubbin (or McKubin), owner of a modest tobacco plantation nearby. Although Maccubbin tore down the old mill and erected a new one sometime between 1792 and '95, he never received title to the land because he failed to complete payment to Benson—who had died in 1790—or to Benson's heirs. In 1804 Benson's daughter and son-in-law complained that Maccubbin was cutting down timber on the property, and later they filed a suit to eject Maccubbin, who told the court that the Benson clan had "most cruelly swept away all the horses, stock, corn, wheat . . . threatening to turn him and his family out of doors in poverty and distress." After the parties had engaged in legal sparring for several years, a jury was empaneled and ruled that Maccubbin owed the Bensons £3,499 plus 5,254 pounds of tobacco (frequently used as a cash substitute). Maccubbin could not pay, and on September 2, 1807, a court-appointed trustee advertised the property for sale in the *Federal Gazette & Baltimore Daily Advertiser,* where it was described as a plantation of 488 acres "with a large and commodious mill house 38 feet by 42, three stories high, one story of which is stone and two of brick . . . ." The mill had two water wheels, three pairs of millstones, and two bolting clothes, one for making fine-grade "merchant" flour (that is, market quality), the other for making coarser "country" flour. The property also included a sawmill, a stable, a smith's shop, a dwelling, and a store house. When the trustee's sale was completed in 1808, the proceeds fell slightly short of the amount of the judgment against Maccubbin, who was ruined

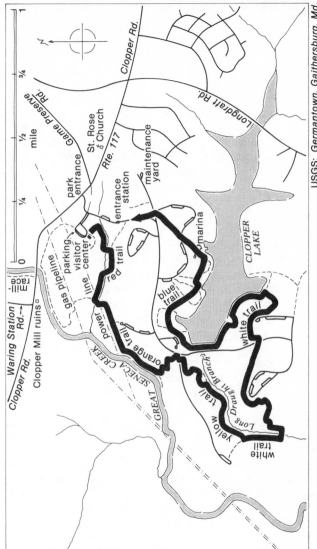

USGS: *Germantown, Gaithersburg, Md.*

and left the vicinity. The purchasers were the Benson heirs, who in 1812 sold the mill and 541 acres for $7,000 to Francis Cassatt Clopper.

Born in Baltimore in 1786, Clopper had already achieved business success as a tobacco merchant in Philadelphia, but he abandoned trade in order to take up the life of a country gentleman and mill owner. Clopper undoubtedly improved the Maccubbin mill, and he may even have rebuilt it; a stone marked "F.C.C. 1834" was set in the wall, and unlike the description in the 1807 advertisement, the surviving ruins of Clopper Mill have two stories of stone and only one of brick. In any case, the operation was run by a series of resident millers, one being Charles Mansfield, who on May 8, 1857, announced in the Rockville *Sentinel* that he was removing from the F.C. Clopper Mill and wished his creditors would settle with him. A year later Richard H. Bennett advertised wool carding at the mill. In 1863 Clopper deeded the mill and Good Part to his married daughter, Mary Augusta Hutton, but retained a life interest for himself and for a spinster daughter, who was to receive half of the "tolls of the mill and mill seat . . . including the tenements now on the right bank of the mill race."

Judging from advertisements, the period of greatest activity at Clopper Mill was between 1850 and 1880. It is not known when the mill stopped operating. An old photograph of the mill shows a stone and brick structure topped by a peaked roof with clapboard gables; four millstones lie on the ground in front, perhaps a sign that the building was no longer used for milling. Although the mill burned in 1947, the gutted ruins still stand. The mill walls, in places three stories high, are visible from Clopper Road across from the intersection with Waring Station Road, about half a mile west of the park entrance (see the map). Part of the millrace still runs along the west bank of the river a few hundred yards upstream from the Clopper Road bridge, and the tailrace is discernible below the mill.

In 1814 Francis C. Clopper bought another mill two miles upstream from Clopper Road. Called Middlebrook Mill, it had been built about twenty years earlier by Abraham Faw, who on May 12, 1794, advertised the works in the *Maryland Journal* as a newly-built merchant gristmill with four pairs of stones "on the most powerful and constant stream in the county." At that time, the property of 240 acres also included a sawmill, a tavern, a store, and a blacksmith's shop.

Clopper also owned a small woolen factory, probably located west of Long Draught Road on land that is now submerged under Clopper Lake. Before the reservoir was created, a millrace and mill ruins were visible. The 1850 census listed the Francis C. Clopper Woolen Manufactory as a water-powered operation with seven employees and a monthly payroll of $125. The works included three looms and various carding machines, fulling stocks, pickers, and spinning frames. The Clopper Woolen Manufactory reportedly made blankets during the Civil War.

Clearly, F.C. Clopper was a man of considerable means and business enterprise. As a farmer he probably grew some tobacco but mostly wheat for his own merchant mills. Archbishop Ambrose Maréchal of Baltimore met Clopper on October 9, 1823, and described him in his diary as a "rich miller whose wife and children are Catholics." In 1847 Clopper gave the land for construction of St. Rose of Lima Church, located on Clopper Road a short distance east of the park entrance. He designed the Rockville courthouse, built in 1840 and torn down fifty years later. Toward the end of his life, he helped to organize a corporation for building a railroad through Montgomery County; when the company failed in 1857 without making much progress, Clopper interested the Baltimore & Ohio Railroad in the project, leading ultimately to construction of the Metropolitan Branch, linking Hagerstown and Georgetown via Frederick. The line passed through Clopper's land a short distance upstream from Clopper Mill, and the local station, for which he donated the land, was named for him, as was the surrounding neighborhood. Clopper died in 1868, and he and his wife and many of their descendants are buried in the graveyard behind St. Rose Church.

Clopper's house was called Woodlands. It formerly stood in the weedy clearing immediately west of the present-day visitor center and park office. The oldest part, built before 1800, was merely a two-story log structure covered with stucco, but in 1812 Clopper constructed a brick and stucco addition that was substantially larger and more elegant than the original house. Following Clopper's death, his daughter Mary Augusta Hutton came into possession. Her husband, William Rich Hutton, was an engineer of note, serving from 1869 to 1874 as Chief Engineer of the C & O Canal. During other periods he was involved in canal, bridge, aqueduct, and railroad projects throughout the mid-Atlantic states and New York. It is not clear how much time Hutton spent at Woodlands, but he died there in 1901 and, like his parents-in-law and his wife, is buried in the graveyard at St. Rose Church. Several unmarried Hutton children, including a son who farmed the estate, lived at Woodlands all their lives. Other descendants occupied the house until it was acquired by the state of Maryland. Left vacant, the house was vandalized and burned in part, then torn down.

Traces of the homestead are evident in the immediate vicinity of the visitor center. For example, a number of ornamental shrubs and spring bulbs compete with the weeds and brush at the edge of the woods. The painted crosswalk at the end of the parking lot nearest the visitor center points directly toward a large linden tree, at the foot of which a millstone, brought up the hill from Clopper Mill by Clopper's grandson, is set into the ground. Behind the millstone are several old, large boxwood bushes, and to the left is a hand-dug well now obscured by thick brush. Across the drive from the linden tree and millstone is a homelike touch: a massive oak with two hooks for a children's swing protruding from a lower branch. In the woods just behind the visitor center there is a log smokehouse chinked with stones, and to the left of the visitor center a series of four terraces that once were flower and vegetable gardens descend into the woods. A water wheel about six feet in diameter sits mired in the bed of a nearby stream; the wheel once powered a pump that lifted water up to the house, which even in the mid-nineteenth century had interior plumbing. Scattered in other spots around the house site and throughout the park are pieces of old farm machinery. Former farm lanes are in places followed by the walk described below. For the most part the route is through forest, but it is obvious that large areas are new growth where fields and meadows have only recently reverted to woods.

AUTOMOBILE: From Exits 35 or 38 of the Capital Beltway (I-495) northwest of Washington, take I-270 toward Frederick about 11 miles to the exit for Route 124 west to Darnestown. From the bottom of the exit ramp, follow Route 124 west 0.5 mile to a crossroads with Route 117 (Clopper Road). Turn right onto Route 117 and go 1.5 miles to the entrance to Seneca Creek State Park on the left. Follow the entrance road a hundred yards, then turn right onto a side road leading to a parking lot by the visitor center.

WALK: Facing the entrance to the visitor center, turn left and follow a wooden walkway around the side of the building and down a stairs. Make a U-turn to the left below a stone retaining wall, then descend into the woods on the Old Pond Trail, which is marked with red blazes. Follow the trail through the woods and along a small stream, which the trail soon crosses. At a T-intersection, turn right onto an overgrown farm lane. Where the lane ends, continue straight on a footpath, which re-enters mature woods, then descends obliquely toward the right and back across the stream. With the brook on the left, continue downstream.

After emerging from the woods at the edge of a right-of-way for a power line, follow the footpath through high weeds to a T-intersection with a rutted road. Turn left and go 20 yards, then bear left again onto an orange-blazed trail leading steeply uphill and along the edge of the right-of-way. Where the transmission lines cross Great Seneca Creek, veer left along the bluff overlooking the river, then descend to the water's edge. With the creek on the right, continue downstream on a trail that at first is rugged, but soon becomes easier.

About 75 yards before a large rock slopes prominently into the creek from the left bank, veer half-left uphill on the orange-blazed trail. Follow the trail as it zigzags uphill and emerges at a road intersection.

Cross the road that intersects from the right. Dive into the woods on the yellow-blazed Long Draught Trail, which at first runs parallel with the road toward the right, then zigzags downhill. Near the bottom of the slope, continue on the yellow-blazed trail as it detours right slightly uphill, then down again to the bottomland. Bear right and follow the yellow-blazed trail through the woods, now and again near Long Draught Branch. At times the trail passes through former fields and pasture, now choked with new growth.

Eventually, turn left at a T-intersection. Follow the white-blazed Mink Hollow Trail along the side of the valley, then left across a bridge over Long Draught Branch. About 40 yards past the bridge, turn left along the foot of the slope. Go 80 yards, then bear right up a tributary ravine. Follow the white-blazed trail uphill, then along the crest of the bluff, with the slope falling off toward the left. After the trail curves right, pass a parking lot in the distance toward the right. Continue on the white-blazed trail through woods and thickets to a park road.

Cross the road obliquely toward the right and re-enter the woods on the white-blazed path. Follow the trail as it zigzags uphill. Continue on the white-blazed trail through the woods, past shelters and a parking lot on the right, then downhill through the woods to Clopper Lake.

At Clopper Lake, turn left along the water's edge. With the lake on the right, follow the white-blazed trail along the shore, except that at one point, about 20 yards before a small indentation in the shoreline, the trail detours left around the mouth of a gully, then returns to the water's edge. Cross the grassy spillway and continue along the shore to the dam.

Turn right across the dam. At a gap in the railing at the far end, turn right onto the Lake Shore Trail, which climbs to a parking lot. Continue below the parking lot, passing a steep trail intersecting from the right. (Despite its name, the Lake Shore Trail follows the shore at a very considerable distance.) For 60 yards follow the blue-blazed Lake Shore Trail along the hillside above a field and the lake, then bear half-right across a weedy field and into the woods. At another clearing, pass straight through a four-way trail intersection. Continue along the edge of a field, through another strip of woods, and straight across another field on a path that is sometimes mowed and sometimes not. With the lake toward the right, continue through woods and fields to a marina.

At the marina follow the left shoulder of a road uphill away from the lake. At a T-intersection, continue across a road and a small footbridge over a drainage ditch. Follow a footpath half-right uphill to a crossroads. At the crossroads, turn left toward the park exit (a gate is visible in the distance). Again, walk on the left shoulder, well off the road. Follow the road past the gate and a parking lot. Turn left onto a road leading to the visitor center.

15

LITTLE BENNETT REGIONAL PARK

Walking or ski touring — 5 miles (8 kilometers). From Hyattstown Mill follow a gravel road along the valley of Little Bennett Creek, at one point fording the stream. Return along a wooded ridge. Because the route described here is, in part, used by automobiles, the best time for a walk is morning, when few cars are present. Also, because the route fords Little Bennett Creek, you may prefer to go in warm weather. Open daily from dawn until dusk. Managed by the Department of Parks, Montgomery County, Maryland-National Capital Park and Planning Commission (301) 972-9222; if no answer, call 972-6581 or 9458. Telephone for information about camping and hunting. The route described here, however, does not cross areas where hunting is allowed.

LITTLE BENNETT REGIONAL PARK typifies Maryland's Piedmont region: a branching system of minor streams — in this case Little Bennett Creek and several of its tributaries — has carved the Piedmont upland into a landscape of rolling hills and low, rounded ridges. Although there are no dramatic rapids or falls, the streams have sufficient gradient and volume to have powered a series of mills built during the eighteenth and nineteenth centuries. This walk passes the sites of two of these works, where in one instance water-driven milling continued well into the twentieth century.

The principal operation along Little Bennett Creek was the Hyattstown Mill, which still stands on the south side of Hyattstown

Mill Road a few hundred yards east of the intersection with Frederick Road. A gristmill and sawmill were first built here sometime between 1783 and 1794 by William Richards on land purchased from Jesse Hyatt, who laid out Hyattstown at the turn of the century. The mill property changed hands frequently during the first half of the nineteenth century. By 1850 George W. Darby, a tenant-miller, was operating the business with the aid of one employee. According to the census of that year, the mill had two pairs of buhrstones and one saw. Annual output was six thousand bushels of meal and thirty-five thousand feet of lumber. An advertisement of sale that appeared in the Montgomery County *Sentinel* on October 8, 1858, provides a more detailed description of the mill:

> 25 Acres of Land, more or less, improved by one large Frame DWELLING HOUSE, one small Dwelling House, one FLOURING MILL, 2 pair of 4 feet burs, new, and all the latest improvements for a Merchant Mill, 1 Country Mill, 1 pair of 3 feet, 7 inch burs, all new machinery; 1 SAW MILL, connected with the Merchant and Country Mill.

The term "mill" does not refer to separate structures but to different machinery for specific tasks; all the apparatus, with the possible exception of the sawmill, was housed in the same building. The two pairs of buhrstones and other "latest improvements" that constituted the flouring mill or merchant mill produced high quality flour for sale on a commercial basis, while the country mill ground corn or other grain on demand for local farmers. At such country mills — also called custom mills — the miller typically retained part of what he ground as a toll or fee for his services, whereas the grain for merchant milling typically was purchased outright by the miller.

The 1858 advertisement did not lead to a sale but five years later the property changed hands at an auction ordered by the Circuit Court of Montgomery County to pay the owner's debts. In 1868 the mill again was sold by court-appointed trustees, whose

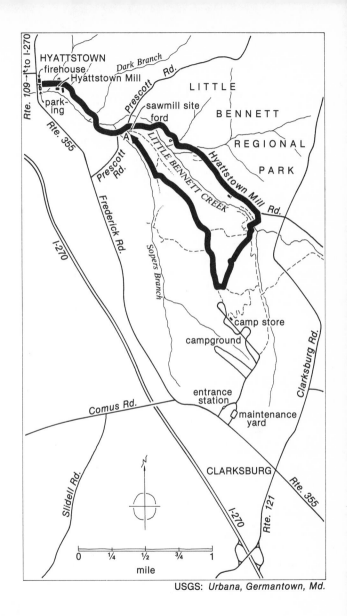

USGS: *Urbana, Germantown, Md.*

handbill described the property as "16 acres of land on Bennett's Creek a little southeast of the village of Hyattstown and 6 miles from the B & O RR. Improved by a 1st rate grist and saw mill with an excellent water power capable of driving two sets of burrs . . . ." The advertisement also listed a comfortable dwelling house containing eight rooms, a miller's house containing five rooms, a large barn, a carriage house, and a "meat house with a never failing spring of pure water convenient to the buildings."

The high bidder, at $2,901, was George A. Darby, perhaps the son of the tenant-miller in 1850. In any case, Darby owned and operated the mill until 1905. The G. M. Hopkins atlas of Montgomery County, published in 1879, shows Darby's gristmill, sawmill, and residence, and also carries an advertisement for George A. Darby, Miller: "Dealer in Flour, Meal, Buckwheat Flour, Feed and Grain of all kinds & Lumber." The 1880 census valued annual output at Darby's mill at $9,160. Business was divided evenly between commercial flour production and custom milling. A fourteen-foot fall of water drove an overshot wheel five feet wide at five revolutions per minute, enabling the mill to grind up to sixty bushels per day.

After Darby sold the property in 1905, the new proprietor installed a modern steel roller mill. Only one pair of stones was retained for producing cornmeal, stone-ground wheat, and animal feed. Water power was supplemented by a steam engine, housed in a shed next to the mill building. An old photograph dated about 1910 shows a structure very much like that seen today, but covered with clapboard instead of sheet metal. Only a few trees stand nearby, and open fields are visible in the background. A horse-drawn wagon rests outside the large door fronting the road.

In 1911 the mill again changed owners, and the following year it was purchased by Frank L. Mortimer, a machinist, and Charles A. Luhn, a cabinetmaker. In addition to continuing their own trades on the premises, Mortimer and Luhn operated the mill. According to the recollections of Charles R. Murphy, who started work at the flour mill about 1914, Mortimer and Luhn purchased outright most of the grain that they processed. They produced cornmeal, whole wheat flour, and a higher grade of baker's flour from which the bran and other coarse particles had been removed by bolting. The firm had its own truck for distributing its flour and cornmeal to stores throughout the area. Some custom milling of animal feed and flour was still done on a fee basis, either for cash or for 25 percent of the finished product. The basement of the mill contained the cog pit or gears for the water-driven stones; the first floor held the stones and the rollers; and the second and third floors contained storage bins, belt-and-bucket elevators for moving the grain through the milling process, and other machinery. According to Mr. Murphy, during periods of persistent rain or high humidity, the corn and wheat on the top floors had to be aired by running the grain up and down the elevators.

In 1918 the mill burned, as reported in the *Sentinel* for September 6:

> Fire, supposed to have originated in the engine room, destroyed the Hyattstown Roller Mills, owned and operated by Mortimer & Luhn, Thursday morning of last week, causing a loss of about $12,000. A barn across the road was also destroyed and a number of horses were endangered. The flames were discovered by a colored woman after such progress had been made that nothing could be done to save the structure or its contents. About 1,000 bushels of wheat and a quantity of corn, flour and a new equipment of machinery were made a total loss. The mill had been operated by its owners for six years . . . . The livestock and other contents of the barn were saved. An insurance of about one-fourth the value of the mill and contents is reported.

Despite the loss, Mortimer and Luhn rebuilt the mill. They dismantled a warehouse from Price's Distillery (namesake of Price's Distillery Road to the east of the park), then used the lumber to reconstruct their mill on the old foundation. On the outside, at least, the new structure closely resembled the old mill, except that the building was sheathed in corrugated metal siding —

169

as can be seen today — that formerly covered the warehouse. New mill machinery was purchased from a manufacturer in Kentucky.

For a few years after its reconstruction, the Hyattstown Mill enjoyed moderate prosperity, but business began to decline during the 1920s as larger mills, located on the railroad in Germantown and Rockville, overshadowed the Hyattstown operation. For decades wheat production in Maryland and other Eastern states had been shrinking, and unless mills were located to receive shipments by rail from the Middle West, they were reduced to grinding out cornmeal or to "corn crushing" for animal feed.

Mortimer and Luhn sold the Hyattstown Mill in 1928. Five years later another sale occurred, for which the advertisement stated, "The mill has been in operation up until this time and has a well established business. It is noted for the fine quality of its water ground corn meal." Operations continued for a period, probably lasting until the late 1930s or early '40s. In 1966 the property was purchased by the Maryland-National Capital Park and Planning Commission for inclusion in Little Bennett Regional Park.

Since the mill is now locked and its windows are boarded, the interior is not visible. Behind the mill is the wheel pit, from which the trench of the tailrace extends toward Hyattstown. The miller's house still stands just up the road, where a millstone is set into the earth in front of the porch. Several hundred yards beyond the miller's house, the ditch and berm of the millrace come into view below Hyattstown Mill Road. The race follows the road for about half a mile to the site of the former millpond. Apparently the dam was located just downstream from the confluence of Dark Branch and Little Bennett Creek. According to the Mortimer & Luhn employee mentioned earlier, the millpond was ten to twelve feet deep at the dam, and covered five to seven acres of what is now low, swampy land north of Hyattstown Mill Road where it intersects with Prescott Road.

This road intersection also marks the site of another old mill. Referring to the map, Prescott Road actually joins Hyattstown Mill Road at two junctions about 160 yards apart. Between the two intersections (but near the more easterly one), a shallow ditch extends south thirty yards to a stone headwall. The ditch is the former tailrace and the wall a fragment of the mill foundation for David A. Zeigler's sawmill and bone mill, shown on Simon Martinet's 1865 map of Montgomery County and again in 1879 on the G. M. Hopkins county atlas. Zeigler's property included a farm of three hundred acres. The sawmill may have been an attempt to exploit the forested ridges in the vicinity; the bone mill ground animal bones for fertilizer. The Zeigler millrace runs east next to Hyattstown Mill Road, then curves off to the south along the side of the hill to join Little Bennett Creek at the former dam site about 180 yards upstream from the present-day ford.

Finally, the G. M. Hopkins atlas shows more mills farther upstream along Little Bennett Creek. Lee Wilson's sawmill stood just below the intersection of Hyattstown Mill Road and Clarksburg Road. Luther G. King's distillery, sawmill, and "old mill" were located in King's Valley, about two miles above the Wilson sawmill. King placed an advertisement in the Hopkins atlas declaring that he was a "Manufacturer and Dealer in Pure Rye and Common Whiskey." The 1880 census valued King's distillery at $6,000, with two employees and output worth $3,888 over a six-month season. Thirty years earlier the census had said that his gristmill, with one pair of stones and one employee, produced eight hundred bushels of meal annually and his sawmill twelve thousand feet of lumber. By 1880, when his gristmill was not mentioned in the census, King may have been grinding rye and corn exclusively for use in his own distillery.

AUTOMOBILE: From Exits 35 or 38 of the Capital Beltway (I-495) northwest of Washington, take I-270 toward Frederick about 22 miles. Pass the exit for Route 121, with its sign indicating Little Bennett Regional Park; instead, continue to the next exit for Route 109 to Barnesville and Hyattstown. From the bottom of the exit ramp, turn left toward Hyattstown. Go 0.4 miles, then turn right onto Route 355 (Frederick

Road). Follow Frederick Road merely a hundred yards, then turn left onto Hyattstown Mill Road just beyond a firehouse. Turn right immediately into a parking lot opposite the end of the firehouse. Although a number of Montgomery County vehicles may be parked in the lot, it is intended also for park users.

WALK: With the firehouse on the left and a children's play lot on the right, follow Hyattstown Mill Road away from Frederick Road. (Walk on the left shoulder in order to minimize the risk of being hit by a car approaching from behind.) Go 275 yards to Hyattstown Mill, a barnlike structure covered with sheet metal.

From the mill, continue on Hyattstown Mill Road past the miller's house and (eventually) above the remains of the millrace next to the road on the right. Follow the road across Dark Branch and Little Bennett Creek, near the site of the former milldam. Continue along the road to a junction where Prescott Road intersects from the right. Bear half-left to continue on Hyattstown Mill Road. Pass a gate (marked A on the map) where a dirt road emerges from the woods on the right. Continue 20 yards to the remains of the tailrace of Zeigler's sawmill and bone mill on the right; a fragment of the stone foundation is visible at the far end of the ditch.

Bear right to continue on Hyattstown Mill Road past another intersection with Prescott Road. (Notice the berm and ditch of the Zeigler headrace running parallel with the road on the right.) Continue to a ford across Little Bennett Creek. Do not attempt to wade across if the stream is higher than your ankles; if it is, return to point A, then turn left for a hike to the campground and back.

After crossing Little Bennett Creek, continue along Hyattstown Mill Road. Pass various parking and picnic areas, a ballfield, and a house. About 60 yards after the road bends abruptly half-left, bear right off the road and onto a grassy horse and hiker trail.

Follow the trail as it turns right across a level valley. Pass a trail intersecting from the right, then cross Little Bennett Creek on a footbridge. Immediately after crossing the bridge, turn left upstream. Go 30 yards, then bear half-right, passing another trail intersecting from the right. Go 70 yards, then fork left. Go 55 yards, then fork right on a well-defined trail that climbs through scrub and pines. (According to a sign present in 1985, this is the Beaver Valley Trail.) As the trail levels off, continue through deciduous woods. At a T-intersection, bear right.

At a T-intersection with a rutted dirt and gravel road, turn right again. Follow the road for a mile along a ridge, straight across a grassy clearing, and through an area of scattered sycamores and new growth. At one point, the trail descends abruptly, then bears right along the hillside. With the slope rising toward the right, continue on the dirt track. At a T-intersection with Hyattstown Mill Road, turn left. Walking on the far left for safety, follow Hyattstown Mill Road back to the starting point.

16

SUGARLOAF MOUNTAIN

Walking — 5 miles (8 kilometers). This isolated mountain offers sweeping views over the Frederick Valley. From the highest parking lot, a short climb leads to the summit. Continue on a loop that follows a ridge across lesser peaks to the north, the returns through the valley of Bear Branch and up another ridge. Dogs must be leashed; camping and fires are prohibited. Motorcycles are not permitted on the mountain road. Open daily from early morning until sunset. The mountain road is closed Christmas and when snow and ice make it impassable. On pleasant afternoons the parking lots and summit attract large crowds, so try to arrive in the morning. Managed by Stronghold, Incorporated; Dickerson, Maryland 20842.

SUGARLOAF MOUNTAIN is a monadnock. Rising eight hundred feet above the surrounding Piedmont upland and still farther above the Frederick Valley to the west, this small but conspicuous mountain is a remnant of a former, higher landscape. (The term *monadnock* is from Mount Monadnock in New Hampshire, left as an isolated eminence by erosion of the region around it.) Sugarloaf stands high while the surrounding land has been worn to a much lower level because the mountain is made of particularly resistant rock. The summit is a massive plate of quartzite composed of grains of quartz sand so solidly cemented together by silica that the rock breaks across the individual grains rather than around them. The quartzite slab that caps the mountain is about two hundred feet thick and is not prone to dissolution,

decay, or chemical disintegration; in consequence, cliffs about 150 feet high have formed around the edges. Below the cliffs are slopes of jumbled, angular boulders (called *talus*), split from the quartzite massif by the expansion of water when it freezes in joints and fissures in the rock.

Underlying the capstone is a softer layer of impure, mica-rich quartzite, slate, and shale about 170 feet thick. Occurring in beds one on top of another, these materials have eroded more quickly than the rock above; they have been cut away to leave a level terrace of soil and loose material buttressed by yet another layer of durable quartzite, similar to the summit slab but not as thick. On the western side of the mountain, part of the terrace is occupied by the parking lot at an elevation of about one thousand feet; the terrace extends around the mountain to the north at a slightly higher elevation and around to the south at a lower level. Again, the quartzite that bolsters the terrace has formed a ring of low cliffs and viewing points.

On a larger scale, Sugarloaf Mountain and the ridge to the north constitute the top of a tight fold of rock strata which, viewed end-on and in cross-section, form an inverted U. Such a downward-opening fold is called an *anticline*. Some geologists assert that the Sugarloaf formation is really the eroded edges of a U-shaped fold opening upward (or *syncline*), but the most recent investigations indicate that whatever synclines occur in the area are lesser folds and minor dimples in the overall anticlinal structure. The top of the anticline peeps above what is now the surface of the earth, and the sides (or *limbs*, as geologists say) plunge beneath the surface to the northwest and southeast, forming a ridge stretching north from the main peak. The rock strata at the north end of the ridge dip beneath the surface, and according to one study, so do the strata at the south end, suggesting that the structure actually consists of an elongated anticlinal dome, now dissected by erosion. Some geologists speculate that the peaks and rock outcrops along the ridge may be areas where deposits of sand that formed the quartzite were thicker or purer (thus creating a more durable stratum of rock) than in areas that now are gaps and saddles

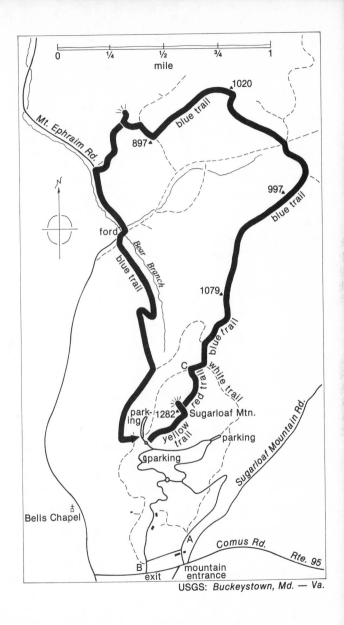

USGS: *Buckeystown, Md. — Va.*

between the peaks. However, a more favored view is that the peaks and outcrops are areas where the strata, originally deposited as horizontal beds of sand, have been crumpled and creased so tightly by pressure exerted from the northwest and southeast that the quartzite layers — now folded over upon themselves — are thicker than they were originally and have thus withstood erosion longer.

There is no knowing what overlying material was worn away in order to expose the Sugarloaf formation, although presumably the sequence and structure of rock strata found at other points in the Piedmont Plateau provide a clue. It is perhaps instructive that at its present level, the floor of the Frederick Valley is formed of soft red sandstone, siltstone, shale, and limestone — all sedimentary rocks that are not particularly resistant to erosion. The Piedmont uplands in the vicinity of Sugarloaf are formed primarily of phyllite, a metamorphic rock intermediate in grade between slate and shist; phyllite is significantly harder than the sedimentary materials of the Frederick Valley but not as durable as quartzite. As for the rate of vertical erosion of the surrounding material, one estimate is a meter each fifty thousand years, indicating that about twelve million years have been required for the Piedmont Plateau to be lowered eight hundred feet from the present height of Sugarloaf peak to the plateau's elevation now. This, however, is little more than a wild surmise.

Sugarloaf Mountain's main peak and the surrounding land belong to Stronghold, Incorporated, a nonprofit corporation organized in 1946 by Gordon Strong, who during the first decades of the century acquired the mountain for a vacation retreat and retirement home. Strong and his sister built houses located at the foot of what is now the exit road. In 1925 Strong considered erecting a planetarium designed by Frank Lloyd Wright on the mountaintop, but then rejected the idea in favor of keeping the area in a more natural state. At the time of Strong's death in 1954, his holdings at Sugarloaf totaled 2,350 acres, which he left to Stronghold, Inc. to be managed as a natural reservation. As of the beginning of 1985, the reservation totaled 3,250 acres. If you want to support the work of Stronghold by making a small contribution, write to Stronghold, Incorporated, P.O. Box 55, Dickerson, Maryland 20842 for a brochure.

AUTOMOBILE: From Exits 35 or 38 of the Capital Beltway (I-495) northwest of Washington, take I-270 toward Frederick about 22 miles to the exit for Route 109 to Barnesville and Hyattstown. From the bottom of the exit ramp, bear right and follow Route 109 toward Sugarloaf Mountain, Comus, and Barnesville. Go 3 miles, then turn right onto Comus Road (state Route 95) toward Sugarloaf Mountain. Follow Comus Road 2.4 miles to a wide, paved area at the mountain entrance. Turn right onto the entrance drive, which passes through a gate. Follow the road steeply uphill. Pass the first large parking lot on the right. Continue along a level stretch of road, then fork right uphill. Immediately past a small traffic circle, turn right into the parking area.

If you want to climb the entire mountain rather than drive most of the way to the top, park near the entrance and use the trail that starts at point A on the map, or take another trail that starts at point B, 30 yards uphill from the foot of the exit road. The climb is not difficult.

WALK: From the rotary or circular drive below the parking lot, follow a flight of stone steps uphill between massive walls. Continue to the summit on a yellow-blazed trail that at first consists of flagstones, then a dirt footpath with log steps, and finally stone stairs.

After touring the summit, pick up the red-blazed trail at the edge of the brush to the north, not far from where the main, yellow-blazed path enters the spacious glade at the top of the mountain. (If you cannot locate the red-blazed trail, return to the rocky high point where the yellow-blazed trail first reaches the summit, then walk toward the glade 35 yards to where red blazes and a footpath appear on the right.)

Follow the red-blazed path downhill to a trail junction (marked C on the map) where a wide, blue-blazed path leads left a few hundred yards to the parking lot. For the longer hike shown on the map, however, turn right at point C onto a narrow footpath marked with both blue and white blazes. Follow the blue and white blazes downhill, then fork left on the blue-blazed trail where the white-blazed path veers right. Continue on the blue-blazed trail through level woods, passing (at a bend in the path) an obscure trail intersecting from the left. Continue through level woods on the blue-blazed path, then uphill to the left. Follow the blue-blazed trail along the side of a ridge, down through a saddle, then up along the ridge again. Descend gradually, at one point passing a path intersecting from the right. Continue to a five-way trail junction.

Cross the trail intersection and continue on the blue-blazed footpath straight uphill, then along the hillside, with the terrain falling off toward the left. Continue as the trail bears right and climbs steeply to another summit. Bear left across the summit, then downhill and along a broad, wooded ridge on the blue-blazed trail. Eventually, turn right where another trail intersects from the left. Follow the blue blazes across the ridge and steeply downhill. About 50 yards after the trail levels off, fork left on the blue-blazed path where another trail veers half-right. Follow the blue blazes along the ridge, then uphill to a minor summit, where a spur trail leads half-right 100 yards to a cliff of white rocks overlooking the Frederick Valley.

With the rocky escarpment toward the right, follow the blue-blazed trail downhill. Continue through woods and downhill to Mt. Ephraim Road. Turn left and follow *the road uphill to an intersection. (Walk on the far left in order to minimize the risk of being hit by a car approaching from behind.) At the intersection, follow the main road to the right for 100 yards, then bear half-left onto a blue-blazed footpath. Follow the path 30 yards, then again fork left to continue on the blue-blazed trail, which climbs gradually away from the road and up the side of a ravine. Continue as the trail switches back and forth uphill and along a wooded ridge. Bear half-right where another trail intersects from the left. Follow the blue-blazed path along the mountainside, then abruptly left uphill. Continue straight through a trail junction. Follow the blue blazes through a boulder field, then steeply uphill to the parking lot.*

17

MARYLAND HEIGHTS

Walking — 5 miles (8 kilometers). A mountain battlefield and citadel. Maryland Heights is the southern end of Elk Ridge, carved into cliffs by the confluence of the Shenandoah and Potomac Rivers at Harpers Ferry. Passing Civil War earthworks, the trail zigzags up the mountainside to the crest of the ridge, where Federal defenders were routed in September 1862. From a stone fort, built after Union forces regained possession of Harpers Ferry, descend on an old military road to the towpath of the C & O Canal. Open daily from dawn until dusk. Managed by the National Park Service. Harpers Ferry office (304) 535-6371.

THE FEDERAL FORTIFICATIONS built atop Maryland Heights during the Civil War were a case of closing the barn door after the horses had got out — or in this case, after Stonewall Jackson and other Confederate war horses had got in. At the outbreak of the war, the Federal arsenal, the C & O Canal, and the tracks, sidings, and depot of the Baltimore & Ohio Railroad — all crowded into the narrow valley at the confluence of the Potomac and Shenandoah Rivers — were guarded by only forty-two Union infantrymen. Virginia seceded from the Union on April 17, 1861, and within two days a thousand armed Virginians led by Rebel militia officers forced the small Federal garrison to evacuate Harpers Ferry. Although the Federals burned the government buildings before they left, the Virginians salvaged a machine for making rifles, as well as several thousand rifle barrels and gun locks, all of which were shipped south.

Soon after seizing Harpers Ferry, the Confederates there were put under the command of Colonel Thomas Jonathan Jackson (later Lieutenant General Stonewall Jackson), who managed to intercept a number of B & O trains, depriving the railroad of 42 locomotives and 386 freight cars. Most of these were wrecked and pushed into the rivers, but 14 locomotives were sent to Richmond, a journey that entailed hauling them by horses along roads for much of the way.

The Confederates stayed at Harpers Ferry for two months, then on June 15 abandoned the town, which they regarded as indefensible. When Union troops reoccupied Harpers Ferry in July, they found, according to one diarist, the "charred ruins were all that remain of the splendid public works, arsenals, workshops and railroads, stores, hotels, and dwelling houses all mingled in one common destruction." By building a pontoon bridge over the Potomac, the Federals reopened the railroad to the West, and for the remainder of 1861 all was quiet at Harpers Ferry.

Late in February 1862, the Union high command decided to stockpile military supplies at Harpers Ferry in preparation for an advance south toward Winchester. But late in May, Stonewall Jackson took the offensive in the Shenandoah Valley, marching to the outskirts of Harpers Ferry before again withdrawing. By late summer the railroad and depot at Harpers Ferry were guarded by 10,400 soldiers, commanded by Colonel Dixon S. Miles, whom a court of inquiry the year before had found to be drunk while leading a division at the first battle of Manassas. (See Chapter 5 for a discussion of First Manassas.) Another 2,500 Union troops were stationed at Martinsburg farther west along the B & O Railroad. Most of these two garrisons had never seen combat, and some units were merely militia; but they and their commander were considered adequate to guard the railroad and canal against Confederate raids.

In September 1862, however, a full-scale Confederate invasion came their way. Following his victory at the second battle of Manassas (see Chapter 6), General Robert E. Lee led his Army of Northern Virginia into Maryland on September 5, wading across

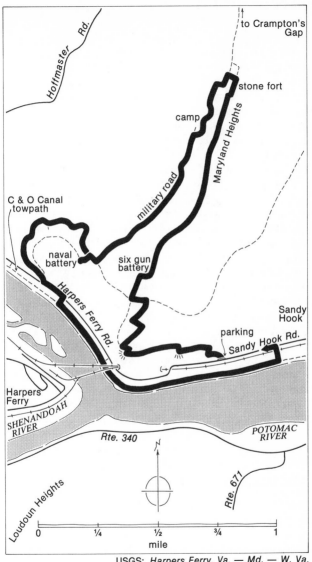

to Crampton's
Gap

stone fort

camp

Maryland Heights

military road

C & O Canal
towpath

naval
battery

six gun
battery

Harpers Ferry Rd.

Sandy
Hook

parking

Sandy Hook Rd.

Harpers
Ferry

SHENANDOAH
RIVER

POTOMAC
RIVER

Rte. 340

Loudoun Heights

Rte. 671

N

| 0 | ¼ | ½ | ¾ | 1 |

mile

USGS: *Harpers Ferry, Va. — Md. — W. Va.*

the Potomac at White's Ford, midway between Washington and Harpers Ferry. Encamped near Frederick, Lee decided on September 9 that before marching farther north into Pennsylvania, as he hoped to do, he should clear his lines of communication to the rear by eliminating the Union garrison at Harpers Ferry. To prevent the Federals from escaping, he devised a plan to approach the town from all sides at once. One Confederate column of about 3,000 men was directed to retrace the army's invasion route, cross the Potomac back into Virginia, and occupy Loudoun Heights, as the ridge overlooking the Shenandoah and the Potomac from the southeast is called. Another Confederate force of about 9,000 men, commanded by Major General Lafayette McLaws, would seize Maryland Heights, which dominates Harpers Ferry from the northeast side of the Potomac. And a third column of about 13,500 men under Stonewall Jackson would march west from Frederick along the National Road, then circle south and east to overrun the Federals' main line of defense on Bolivar Heights west of Harpers Ferry. Once the high ground that towers above Harpers Ferry on all sides was in Southern hands, the Confederates could shell the town and its defenders into submission.

The Union high command had been aware of the threat to Harpers Ferry ever since the Confederates first crossed the Potomac into Maryland. Major General George B. McClellan, commander of the Army of the Potomac, urged that the garrison at Harpers Ferry be withdrawn before it was cut off, but Henry Halleck, general-in-chief of all Union forces, ordered that the town be held. On September 5, Colonel Miles at Harpers Ferry received a telegram from his immediate superior in Baltimore: "Be energetic and active, and defend all places to the last extremity. There must be no abandoning of a post, and shoot the first man that thinks of it, whether officer or soldier." Six days later, as the Confederates closed in on Harpers Ferry, Miles telegraphed to Washington, "I expect this will be the last you will hear of me until this affair is over. All are cheerful and hopeful."

By nightfall on September 12, Lafayette McLaws' Confederate column was poised to seize Maryland Heights. (These heights are not an isolated hill but rather the southern end of a long ridge called Elk Ridge.) McLaws sent two brigades totaling 3,000 men to scale Elk Ridge four miles north of Maryland Heights and then advance south along the wooded ridge. With the rest of his troops, McLaws moved south along the foot of the mountain to seal the eastern exit from Harpers Ferry. Also on September 12, the Federal garrison from Martinsburg arrived in Harpers Ferry, retreating before Stonewall Jackson, who was on the last leg of his approach from the west.

Maryland Heights was the key to the defense of Harpers Ferry. Halfway up the southwestern slope, and directly across the Potomac from the town, a powerful gun emplacement called the Naval Battery had been erected the preceding May to cover the approaches from the south and west. The guns were formidable: two 9-inch naval Dahlgren rifles, one 50-pounder Parrott rifle, and four 12-pounder smoothbores. The largest guns were far bigger than anything the Confederates had brought with them, and if handled well could destroy the Southern field artillery before it was close enough to fire back. Little, however, had been done to guard against an attack from the north or east, as now was threatened. Except for a log breastwork that had been thrown up at the last minute, the crest of the ridge was unfortified. Both Halleck and McClellan had suggested that the entire garrison at Harpers Ferry withdraw to Maryland Heights, but such a move was not practicable because there was no water on the mountain, nor had cisterns been built. For the defense of the heights, Colonel Miles assigned only 1,600 troops, some of whom had been in the army only three weeks and were still unpracticed at loading their guns.

The attack on Maryland Heights opened at daybreak on September 13. The Yankee recruits were posted in a line of battle about four hundred yards in advance of the makeshift breastwork, and they could hear to their front the Southerners talking and moving in the dim woods and underbrush. Even before the Confederates were seen, their first volley crashed into the defenders. After firing their own rifles into the smoke and woods, the green Federal troops scrambled for the breastwork behind them. There a new line of battle was formed, but when the Confederates advanced and fired another volley, a regiment of raw Union recruits broke and ran. "They were in wild confusion and dismay . . . . Nobody could possibly hold them," a lieutenant of a veteran regiment later testified. As the veterans tried to form a new line, the rookies took shelter to their rear. One officer saw three men trying to hide behind a single tree.

Colonel Thomas H. Ford, the Federal commander at Maryland Heights, sent a dispatch to Colonel Miles in Harpers Ferry saying that one regiment had all run, and that his own troops were out of ammunition. "I must leave the hill unless you direct otherwise," Ford reported. Miles came up to the heights to see, but when Ford pleaded for reinforcements, Miles told him, "You can't have another damned man. If you can't hold it, leave it." Ford tried to hold on, but his small force was outnumbered. The Union troops were pushed back from the north and east, and soon Ford ordered an evacuation. After spiking the guns in the Naval Battery or pushing them down the mountainside, the Federals crossed the pontoon bridge over the Potomac River and joined the rest of the trapped garrison in Harpers Ferry.

By now the Confederate encirclement of Harpers Ferry was complete. Maryland Heights was in their hands; two Southern brigades occupied the crest of Loudoun Heights, which they had found undefended; and Stonewall Jackson's large force was drawn up opposite the Federal positions on Bolivar Heights. During the night of September 13, ten Union cavalry troopers broke out from the besieged town and managed to carry a verbal message from Colonel Miles to General McClellan, who had advanced with the Army of the Potomac from Washington to Frederick. McClellan was told that the Harpers Ferry garrison could hold out for forty-eight hours, but that if the town was not relieved in that time, Miles would have to surrender. McClellan replied with a dispatch saying that help was on the way. "Hold out to the last extremity," he told Miles. "If it is possible, reoccupy the Maryland Heights with your whole force." This message was carried by three separate couriers, but none got through. As for the promised help, the prior afternoon McClellan had, in fact, ordered Major General William B. Franklin, commanding a force of 19,500 men, to break the siege at Harpers Ferry by advancing against the Confederates who were pressing the town from the northeast, but Franklin had not gotten under way until the next morning, September 14.

Meanwhile, the Confederates spent the morning of the 14th getting their guns into position on the high ground surrounding Harpers Ferry. On Loudoun Heights five rifled fieldpieces were in place by noon, with all Harpers Ferry within range. At Maryland Heights the track along the ridge was impassable by artillery, so a shorter path was cut up the mountainside from the east. Ropes were tied to four fieldpieces, and with as many as two hundred men on each gun, the artillery was dragged up to the crest. At the same time, Jackson seized positions from which to rake the Union defenses that still remained on Bolivar Heights.

Early in the afternoon, the Confederate guns on Loudoun Heights and Maryland Heights opened fire. "Their shells at first fell far wide of the mark and we laughed at them," a Union cavalryman wrote later, "but they soon got the range and plumped shell after shell among us, hitting a few horses and causing a rush for cover." Another man recalled, "*The infernal screech owls* came hissing and singing, then bursting, plowing great holes in the earth, filling our eyes with dust, and tearing many giant trees to atoms." Union gunners tried to reply, but the battery on Maryland Heights was out of range and the Confederates on Loudoun Heights suffered only four casualties.

The next morning, September 15, the Confederates resumed their bombardment. Jackson's guns to the west joined in the action, and the Federal lines on Bolivar Heights were shelled from all directions. By 8 A.M. the Union artillery had stopped firing in return, and shortly afterwards, as Jackson's troops prepared to charge, the Federals surrendered, sending a horseman forward with a white flag. Even so, several minutes passed before word reached all the Confederate batteries, many of which continued to lob shells at the Union positions. Among the last casualties was Colonel Miles, who received a mortal wound in the leg.

Meanwhile, that same morning, the Federal relief column under William Franklin arrived to the east of Elk Ridge, where the Yankees encountered 5,000 Confederates. The Southerners appeared to be caught in a vise between the garrison at Harpers Ferry and Franklin's 19,500 troops. But as Franklin pondered whether to attack, cheering was heard from the Confederate lines, and word soon reached the Federals that Harpers Ferry had surrendered. Early in the afternoon, the Confederates withdrew rapidly around the southern end of Maryland Heights and entered the captured town, joining forces with Stonewall Jackson.

Except for 1,300 Union cavalrymen who had managed to break out of Harpers Ferry during the previous night, the entire Federal garrison was captured. The prisoner count came to over 11,500, a figure so disturbing that when the news was released to the Northern press, censors in the War Department cut the figure in half to reduce the public's outrage. Captured war material included 73 pieces of artillery, 13,000 rifles and other small arms, 200 wagons, and abundant supplies of all kinds. New Springfield rifles were distributed to Southern regiments that previously had old smoothbores, and Confederate recruits who had marched for days with no guns at all were armed.

By evening on the 15th, most of the Confederate troops had left Harpers Ferry, heading north along the Potomac to Sharpsburg, where General Lee and the rest of his army were drawn up behind Antietam Creek, awaiting attack by the Army of the Potomac. At Harpers Ferry, only Major General A.P. Hill's Confederate division remained behind to organize a wagon train to carry the booty to Richmond. Even Hill's troops abandoned the town after only two days, leaving early on the morning of the battle of Antietam. Marching seventeen miles in eight hours, they arrived at Sharpsburg in time to turn back an attack that threatened Lee's entire position. (See Chapter 18 for a discussion of the battle of Antietam.)

After the bloody stand-off at Antietam Creek, Lee withdrew into Virginia, and Harpers Ferry changed hands for the fourth time of the war as Federal troops returned. In response to what quickly was dubbed the Harpers Ferry fiasco, measures were taken to strengthen the defenses. All trees on the upper third of Maryland Heights were cut down. In October 1862, a substantial earthwork mounting six 30-pounder Parrott rifles and two 24-pounder siege guns was constructed high up the ridge to sweep Loudoun and Bolivar Heights and other approaches from the south and west. Spanning the entire crest farther north, a masonry and earthen fort was built to block attack along the ridge or mountain flanks. Powder magazines, breastworks, and an infantry encampment with cisterns to collect rain were prepared for a possible siege. Traces of these works are still visible along the route described at the end of the chapter.

During Lee's second invasion of the North in June 1863, the Confederate army forded the Potomac twelve miles upstream from Harpers Ferry. The town's garrison withdrew to Maryland Heights, then was ordered to join the Army of the Potomac as it passed north up the Frederick Valley to intercept Lee's march toward Harrisburg, Pennsylvania. For a brief period Southern troops guarding Lee's lines of communication occupied Harpers Ferry and the abandoned works on the mountain, but after Lee's defeat at Gettysburg early in July, the Confederates retreated to Virginia.

A year later the Union garrison at Harpers Ferry again evacuated the town and withdrew to Maryland Heights during Major General Jubal Early's sudden march across Maryland and thrust at Washington. This time, however, the Federals waited out the invasion behind their defenses atop the mountain. The Southerners were in a hurry, and after some skirmishes and exchange of artillery fire, Early decided that the defenses were too strong to take quickly. Bypassing the Union position, he continued toward Washington, reaching its outskirts on the same day that Union reinforcements arrived in the capital to turn back his attack. Early's raid was the last gasp of Southern offensive effort in the East, and for the rest of the war Harpers Ferry and the defenses on Maryland Heights saw no action.

*AUTOMOBILE: From Exits 35 or 38 of the Capital
Beltway (I-495) northwest of Washington, take I-270
toward Frederick. As you approach Frederick, exit onto
I-70 west toward Hagerstown. After merging with I-70,
go only 0.5 mile, then exit onto Route 340 west toward
Charles Town (the exit is also marked Route 15 south
toward Leesburg). Follow Route 340 for 15.2 miles to
an exit for Route 180 opposite Valley Road. Turn left
onto Route 180 and go uphill 0.2 mile, then turn right
onto Sandy Hook Road. Follow Sandy Hook Road
downhill and along the railroad for 1.2 miles to a
narrow, informal parking area at the right shoulder of
the road, where a flight of stone steps climbs the slope.
(If you cross over the railroad, you have driven 0.2
miles too far.)*

*To visit Harpers Ferry at the end of your hike, return
to Route 340, then follow it left downhill and across the
Potomac River. Continue almost 2 miles. After crossing
another bridge over the Shenandoah River, turn right
immediately into Harpers Ferry National Historical
Park.*

*WALK: The trail is marked with orange blazes. Follow
the stone stairs steeply uphill about 35 steps, then
continue straight along the hillside, with the Potomac
River toward the left. Follow the orange-blazed trail as it
zigzags uphill. Pass a rocky viewpoint and continue
uphill along the mountainside to the top of the cliffs
overlooking Harpers Ferry and the confluence of the
Potomac and Shenandoah Rivers.*

*From the overlook opposite Harpers Ferry, continue
a few dozen yards uphill away from the town, then bear
left along the slope for a short distance. Just beyond
another viewpoint, turn sharp right uphill on the
orange-blazed trail. With the slope falling off toward the
right, follow the trail on a long traverse uphill. Continue*

as the trail zigzags up to a dirt road. Turn left and follow the road 160 yards to a trail intersection. Turn right and follow the footpath straight uphill to an overgrown earthwork where the six-gun battery was located.

Turn right immediately in front of the ditch and earth bulwark of the six-gun battery. With the battery toward the left, continue along the footpath, which soon veers uphill. (The trail is marked with both orange and blue blazes.) Continue uphill, then follow a ridge past the pits of old, collapsed powder magazines and the site where a 100-pounder Parrott rifle was mounted. Continue along the ridge to the stone fort.

The ruins of the stone fort reflect the likelihood that it was never finished and that after the war it served as a quarry for pre-cut rock. The fort was part of a larger work spanning the entire mountaintop. Earth breastworks are still discernible extending across the ridge slightly north of the masonry citadel. The main line of defense was pierced with embrasures for seven light field guns and one 30-pounder Parrott rifle. To improve visibility, the entire area was stripped of trees, which were used to make abatis — or that is, infantry obstacles formed by aligning the trunks toward the fort, with the branches outward. Large pits that once were powder magazines are visible within the perimeter. The magazines originally had timber roofs covered with six to ten feet of earth. A 100-pounder Parrott rifle weighing nearly five tons was mounted about a thousand yards south of the fort where it could fire in any direction.

From the stone fort, continue along the ridge 25 yards beyond the fort, then turn left on the orange-blazed path. (The blue-blazed trail continues north 10 miles to Crampton's Gap.) Follow the orange-blazed path more or less straight 85 yards to a low stone wall; this and the earth bulwark visible to the right mark the west and north perimeter of the fort. Turn left; with the wall on the right, continue to a corner of the fort. Cross the wall and follow the orange-blazed path downhill past a stone breastwork, then bear left along a level area. Follow the trail as it winds through the woods and past the site of the military camp.

Turn left onto the old military road. With the slope falling off to the right, follow the dirt road downhill along the mountainside. At a T-intersection, turn right downhill. After about 120 yards, a footpath leads left steeply downhill 160 yards to a rectangular earthwork that was the site of the Naval Battery.

From the Naval Battery, return uphill to the dirt military road and follow it downhill to Harpers Ferry Road next to the C & O Canal ditch. Bear left and follow the left shoulder of the road 300 yards to a footbridge over the canal ditch. With the canal ditch on the left and the Potomac River on the right, follow the towpath past a lock and a lockkeeper's house and under two railroad bridges. Continue on the towpath past a stone dike on the right (an unsuccessful effort to divert floods) and eventually past another ruined lock. About 350 yards below the lock — as rooftops come into view on the left beyond the canal and railroad — turn left onto one of any informal paths; a good one occurs 80 yards past milepost 60. Cross the canal ditch and (with caution) the railroad. With the railroad on the left, follow Sandy Hook Road 300 or 400 yards to the parking area by the stone steps. Walk on the left shoulder of the road in order to minimize the risk of being struck by cars approaching from behind.

18

ANTIETAM NATIONAL BATTLEFIELD

Walking — 2 miles (3.2 kilometers). A rolling landscape of fields and woods, scattered farmhouses, and a few landmarks made famous by the grisly photographs of Mathew Brady and Alexander Gardner: the Dunker Church (reconstructed), Bloody Lane, and the Burnside Bridge. Here, on September 17, 1862, more soldiers died than on any other day of the Civil War. Tour the battlefield by automobile, then stop at the Burnside Bridge, where a short hiking trail leads downstream along Antietam Creek. The trail can be muddy after heavy rain or during periods of thaw, so the best — and most authentic — time for a visit is the dry season during late summer and early fall. Dogs must be leashed. The park is open daily 8:30 A.M. until dusk. The visitor center is open daily, except Thanksgiving, Christmas, and New Year's Day, 8:30 A.M. to 5 P.M. (or later during summer if funds are available). Managed by the National Park Service (301) 432-5124.

A NTIETAM NATIONAL BATTLEFIELD has been developed primarily for automobile sightseeing. Unlike Manassas National Battlefield, with its outstanding opportunities for foot touring (see Chapters 5 and 6), the fields at Antietam lack a comprehensive trail system. The only way to see the battlefield is by car or bicycle along a system of paved roads — although inveterate hikers, of course, can follow the road shoulders. One would think, given the park's mission to foster factual and emotional understanding of the battle, that trails would be

provided for visitors to advance across the fields and slog up the slopes *on foot*, as the soldiers did. But still, an automobile tour through the battlefield is well worthwhile, and at Burnside Bridge there is a short hiking loop. Yet even this trail is in a deteriorated — although still passable — condition because it is no longer maintained by the park service.

The battle of Antietam was an outgrowth of General Robert E. Lee's success at the second battle of Manassas, fought on August 29 and 30, 1862. After pushing the Union army into Washington, Lee decided to carry the war to the North. On September 5 he led his Army of Northern Virginia into Maryland, wading across the Potomac River at White's Ford, midway between Washington and Harpers Ferry. Lee wrote to Jefferson Davis, President of the Confederacy, that by invading Maryland he would at least throw the Federals on the defensive and be able to feed and refit his ragged troops in an area as yet unscathed by the war. He told one of his officers that his goal was Harrisburg, Pennsylvania, where he wanted to burn the Pennsylvania Railroad's bridge over the Susquehanna River. But his ultimate objective was to make a demonstration in Northern territory and thus lure the Union Army of the Potomac, commanded by Major General George B. McClellan, into a showdown. As Lee said after the war, "I went into Maryland to give battle."

Lee already had faced McClellan the prior spring during the Peninsula Campaign, where Lee had learned to exploit the Union general's excessive prudence. Now Lee felt that he could defeat McClellan again and perhaps even destroy a large part of the Federal army, putting the South in a strong position to offer the North an armistice in exchange for independence. He told Davis that the invasion would help convince Northern voters in the impending fall elections to support candidates who favored a settlement accommodating the Confederacy. Also, another victory in the field might provide the occasion for Great Britain and other European powers to recognize the Confederacy as an independent nation and to exert pressure on the North to let the South go its

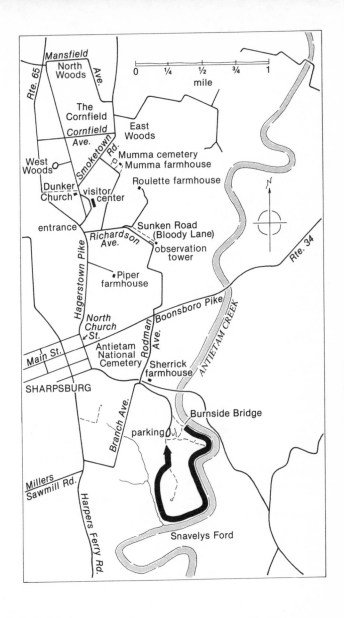

own way. After all, England wanted cotton for its textile industry, which was being hampered by the Federal blockade of Southern ports; nor was the prospect of a weaker Union — the Balkanization of the United States, as we might say today — upsetting to English leaders for whom the pre-eminence of the British empire was the prime consideration.

When Lee entered Maryland, his army numbered about 50,000 men. The Southern soldiers were experienced and self-confident, but after three months on the offensive, they were physically run-down, ill-nourished on a diet of apples and unripe corn, and poorly equipped. Many had no shoes. One Confederate veteran later recalled that the troops were "a set of ragamuffins," and that "it seemed as if every cornfield in Maryland had been robbed of its scarecrows." He continued:

> None had any under-clothing. My costume consisted of a ragged pair of trousers, a stained, dirty jacket; an old slouch hat, the brim pinned up with a thorn; a begrimed blanket over my shoulder, a grease-smeared cotton haversack full of apples and corn, a cartridge box full, and a musket . . . . There was no one there who would not have been "run in" by the police had he appeared on the streets of any populous city.

After crossing the Potomac, Lee rested his army for a few days at Frederick while he pondered what to do next. On September 9 he issued marching orders to his top officers. His plan was to move west of South Mountain (as the extension of the Blue Ridge into Maryland and Pennsylvania is called) and to use the long ridge as a shield behind which to march north toward Harrisburg. But first, in order to secure his lines of communication through the Shenandoah Valley, he had to capture Martinsburg and Harpers Ferry, held by Union garrisons totaling 13,000 men. Three Confederate columns would approach the towns from separate directions, drive the Federals at Martinsburg into Harpers Ferry, then bag the lot while Lee remained with about a third of the Confederate army west of South Mountain. (For a discussion of the capture of Harpers Ferry, see Chapter 17.)

Lee's plan of dividing his army in the face of a numerically superior enemy that was known to be advancing from Washington defied conventional military wisdom, but Lee had used similar tactics to confuse and defeat Major General John Pope at the second battle of Manassas. By the time General McClellan realized what was going on and prepared his response, it would be too late to save Harpers Ferry or to stop Lee from reuniting his army. Then Lee expected to deal with McClellan as opportunity afforded.

McClellan, however, benefited from a freak of fortune: the discovery near Frederick on September 13 of a copy of Lee's order setting forth his entire plan and the route taken by each Confederate column. How the order was lost has never been explained, but the document appeared to be genuine — and was. It clarified what until then had been a series of seemingly contradictory reports on the movements and whereabouts of the Southern army. McClellan was exultant. He foresaw the destruction of Lee's forces one piece at a time. In a letter to President Lincoln, the Union general said, "I think Lee has made a gross mistake, and that he will be severely punished for it. . . . I have all the plans of the rebels, and will catch them in their own trap if my men are equal to the emergency. . . . Will send you trophies."

Yet even extraordinary opportunity could not galvanize McClellan into quick action. On the morning of September 14, nearly seventeen hours after he first read the lost orders, he finally moved the Army of the Potomac forward from Frederick. By that evening the Federals had broken enemy resistance at Turner's Gap and Crampton's Gap on South Mountain, but there the Union army halted for the night while the Confederates prepared to withdraw. Lee sent word to the men besieging Harpers Ferry that he planned to retreat into Virginia and that they should do the same. But then he received a message that Harpers Ferry was expected to fall the next morning (as indeed it did), so he issued new orders directing the scattered Confederate army to join forces at Sharpsburg, where he and the 15,000 troops with him took up positions west of

Antietam Creek on the morning of September 15. Lee deployed his infantry along a wide front, as though they were far more numerous than they really were, then waited for reinforcements. By mid-afternoon the leading units of the Army of the Potomac confronted the Confederates from across the creek, but McClellan was taken in by Lee's bluff and did not attack.

Accounts of the battle of Antietam are replete with recitations of the opportunities and advantages that McClellan let slip through his fingers. Among the more prominent instances is McClellan's failure to press the attack on the afternoon of the 15th, or even the next day, when he had 60,000 troops on hand, outnumbering the Confederates four to one. But McClellan consistently overestimated the size of Lee's army; four days earlier he had told the Union high command in Washington that the Confederates numbered 120,000 men, thus casting himself as the underdog. So McClellan spent September 16 waiting for still more troops to arrive, while those already on hand took up their assigned positions. Meanwhile, most of the Confederate units that had captured Harpers Ferry reached Sharpsburg, swelling the Southern ranks to 35,000 men, with more coming.

Just as surprising as McClellan's reluctance to fight is Lee's willingness. He, at any rate, knew that he was greatly outnumbered. Although his position was strong, stretching in a wide, shallow arc along the brow of the plateau north, east, and south of Sharpsburg, with good roads providing interior lines of communication, he had his back to the Potomac, and if the battle went against him, the river would prevent a quick withdrawal. One can only assume that Lee thought he could win, as he had won before, due to the fighting superiority and tenacity of his veterans, the skill and nerve of his officers, and a not inconsiderable measure of Union incompetence.

By dawn on September 17, McClellan felt that he was ready. If he had a preconceived plan, he had not told anybody, so that as the attack developed, it took on an ill-coordinated and ponderous momentum of its own. Even in his report afterward, McClellan seems to have been somewhat unsure of just what it was he had attempted to do, saying that he had intended "to make the main attack on the enemy's left — at least to create a diversion in favor of the main attack, with the hope of something more by assailing the enemy's right — and as soon as one or both of the flank movements were fully successful, to attack their center with any reserve that I might then have in hand." But as things turned out, there was no main Union attack; instead, the Federal assuault came piecemeal, as has occurred during the first and second battles of Manassas. The Union blows were heavy, but none was a knock-out punch, delivered with the overwhelming power and resources at McClellan's command. The battle became a series of separate engagements, in which different Federal corps attacked, were used up in desperate fighting, and retired. Even as the day wore on and the Confederates appeared to weaken under the successive blows, McClellan held back his ample reserves, fearful of making an all-out commitment.

The battle began at first light as Yankee and Confederate artillerists shelled each other north of Sharpsburg. At sunrise Major General Joe Hooker's First Corps of 8,600 Federals advanced south along both sides of the Hagerstown Turnpike. Hooker had moved into position astride the turnpike the prior afternoon, in full sight of the Confederates, who had adjusted their lines to meet him. Blocking the Union advance was Major General Thomas "Stone-wall" Jackson with 7,700 men, some of them drawn up in a line of battle stretching out from each side of the road, facing north, and the rest held in reserve to the rear. Four Confederate batteries occupied a rise near a plain, whitewashed building called the Dunker Church because its congregation of German Baptist Brethren practiced baptism by total immersion. More Confederate artillery was arrayed to the northwest on Nicodemus Hill, where the guns could rake the advancing ranks of Union infantry.

The Yankees, however, were supported by their own artillery. From the far side of Antietam Creek, long-range, 20-pounder Parrott rifles maintained a steady but inaccurate bombardment. Firing over the heads of the advancing Federals, still more Union artillery occupied a low, wooded ridge called the North Woods farther up the turnpike. These guns blasted the Confederate infantry waiting in a field of head-high corn just east of the turnpike and less than half a mile north of the Dunker Church. This area, afterward called simply *the* Cornfield, became one of the chief killing-grounds of the battle. To its east were the East Woods, which repeatedly changed hands but were eventually held by the Yankees, and to the west, on the far side of the turnpike and behind the Dunker Church, were the West Woods, shielding the Confederate reserves.

By 7 A.M. a general meelee, half-obscured by smoke, covered the area of the Dunker Church, the Cornfield, and the woods to east and west. In a series of surges, retreats, and renewed assaults, the Federals pushed toward the Dunker Church. The casualties on both sides quickly mounted, and men afterward spoke of the "terrible fire," the "fearful and incessant" gunnery, and wondered how they got out alive. Hooker's attack appeared to be succeeding, and the general himself was seen riding from one part of the field to another, urging his men on. But then 2,300 Confederate reinforcements from the division of Brigadier General John Hood poured out of the West Woods, crossed the turnpike, and broke the Yankee spearhead with a volley that was "like a scythe running through our line," according to a Union field officer. The Federal formation faltered, then a gradual but general withdrawal began. The Union troops were beaten back along the turnpike to the North Woods, where their artillery, using double charges of cannister shot, stopped the Confederate counterattack. In the face of this fire, "whole ranks went down," a Yankee officer said, and later the Southern dead were found heaped on top of each other.

The carnage continued unabated. As the First Corps retreated, the Union Twelfth Corps of Major General Joseph Mansfield advanced from the northeast along the Smoketown Road. The Yankees drove the Confederates out of the East Woods and the Cornfield and pushed them west across the turnpike, where the fences were draped with corpses, and out of sight behind the West Woods. The Confederate line in this sector had been facing north, in the direction of Hooker's earlier attack, but now the Confeder-

ANTIETAM NATIONAL BATTLEFIELD

ates regrouped in ranks facing east, reinforced by troops that Lee shifted from his center.

There was a lull in the fighting while the Twelfth Corps waited for support and a third Union attack got under way. At 7:20 A.M. Major General Edwin Summer, commander of the Second Corps, which included three divisions with 5,000 infantry in each, received orders to cross Antietam Creek and join the troops already in battle. Two divisions, one commanded by Major General John Sedgewick and the other by Brigadier General William French, moved out immediately, but the fighting was two miles to their front, and by the time Sedgewick's division, which took the lead, arrived at the East Woods, the attack of the Twelfth Corps was stalled and French's trailing division was nowhere to be seen, having veered off toward the south. Without waiting to consult with the officers of the Twelfth Corps, Sumner deployed Sedgewick's division in three ranks 500 yards wide, one behind the other, then sent them forward. Setting out shortly after 9 A.M. the Federals were at first unopposed and moved west across the Cornfield, but when the Union ranks reached the turnpike, they were hit by artillery fire from the hills to the west. Still the Yankees advanced, entering the West Woods above the Dunker Church. But then 4,400 Confederates, some of them just arrived from Harpers Ferry and others from positions below Sharpsburg, dashed in from the south. In a flanking attack, the Confederates poured volley after volley down the ranks of Union infantry, who broke and retreated north out of the battle after suffering 2,200 casualties. The Confederates pursued, were blasted by the Union artillery at the North Woods, and in turn retreated to the cover of the West Woods, with losses of 40 percent.

With that, most of the fighting at the northern end of the battlefield came to an end, after a morning of nearly constant killing. The Union troops had suffered about 7,000 casualties, and the Confederates about 6,000. Later in the day, some of McClellan's officers urged that he renew the attack at the north end of the field with reinforcements that had arrived during the morning, but McClellan refused. By then he was afraid that Lee was preparing a counterstroke, and he felt that he needed all the reserves on hand for defense.

Meanwhile, the battle had spread farther south. William French's division from the Second Corps had become separated from Sedgewick's division and now French decided to direct his attack toward a road (since termed the Sunken Road or Bloody Lane) that was so worn and eroded that it occupied a shallow trough zigzagging across the Confederate center east of the Hagerstown Turnpike. The road served as a trench for 2,500 Southerners, and as French's division appeared over the rise to their front, the Confederates' first volley brought the Union ranks to a standstill. "The effect was appalling," a Southern officer later reported. "The entire front line, with a few exceptions, went down in the consuming blast." More frontal attacks were tried and failed. A Confederate sergeant described the action as "systematic killing." Recalling the experience of advancing over the brow of the hill, a Yankee soldier wrote:

> An occasional shell whizzed by or over, reminding us that we were rapidly approaching the "debatable ground" . . . . The compressed lip and set teeth showed that nerve and resolution had been summoned to the discharge of duty. A few temporarily fell out, unable to endure the nervous strain, which was simply awful. . . .

For about two hours the Federals were stymied in front of the Sunken Road. Eventually, another Union division of 5,000 men, commanded by Major General Israel Richardson, arrived on the scene. Although Richardson's division was part of the Second Corps, which had gone into combat hours earlier, McClellan had not allowed Richardson to cross Antietam Creek until 9:30 A.M., when reinforcements had arrived to take its place among the reserves. Finally, after another futile frontal assault by the Union troops, the Confederates in the road were outflanked by a Federal brigade that approached from the southeast, where the Yankees could shoot down the length of the lane, which was crowded with infantry. A Confederate soldier wrote, "The slaughter was terrible! When ordered to retreat I could scarcely extricate myself from the dead and wounded around me." Scores of men were shot as they scrambled up the bank behind the road and ran across the field to the rear.

The Confederates pulled back and the fighting continued as the Yankees, advancing now from the Sunken Road, tried to break their enemy's final line of resistance in front of the Hagerstown Turnpike. For the Confederates, the situation was desperate. Their infantry, weakened earlier by the withdrawal of units to bolster positions to the north, had suffered casualties of 30 percent, and those still fit to fight were in disarray. A makeshift line of twenty fieldpieces was all that held the Yankees back. The Union commanders on the scene felt that one more push would split the Confederate center wide open. Richardson asked for artillery support, but was told that no guns were available. McClellan wanted them in reserve or massed to the north in case of a Confederate counterattack there. And so the Union attack petered out, and the Federals pulled back below the Sunken Road.

As the fighting died down in the central area of the battlefield, it intensified in the south, where a stone bridge (later named the Burnside Bridge) crossed Antietam Creek. Major General Ambrose Burnside and Brigadier General Jacob Cox, his field commander, had spent the early part of the morning waiting for orders to send the Union Ninth Corps into battle. This force consisted of four divisions totaling 13,000 men, and it was opposed, in the immediate vicinity of the bridge, by only 400 Georgians. But the Confederate position was strong: the Georgians were concealed in the woods atop a bluff that not only overlooked the bridge but also the road that approached it from the southeast along the opposite bank of the creek. Farther downstream there were another hundred or so Confederates, and up the hill, on the open slopes south of Sharpsburg, Confederate artillery and 3,000 infantry waited to counter a breakthrough at the bridge. Earlier there had been more infantry south of Sharpsburg, but Lee had shifted them north to repel attacks at the opposite end of the Confederate line.

A few minutes before 10 A.M., while Burnside and Cox watched from a distance the start of General French's attack on the Sunken Road, a courier arrived from McClellan with orders directing Burnside to cross the stone bridge. Almost immediately, the Union artillery opened fire in a preliminary bombardment, and then a regiment of Federals moved forward to form a skirmish line along the east side of the creek. But they made easy targets and fell back after a third had been shot. A larger force, which was supposed to storm down the hillside facing the bridge and cross under cover of fire from the skirmishers, got lost in the woods and eventually reached the creek 350 yards upstream, where they stayed, sniping at Confederates on the opposing hillside.

Meanwhile, a Union division under Brigadier General Isaac Rodman was supposed to wade across the creek two-thirds of a mile downstream from the bridge at a ford selected earlier by McClellan's engineers, but the place proved to be unusable because the stream banks and bluff were too steep. So Rodman continued marching downstream, looking for a place called Snavely's Ford that had been mentioned by local farmers.

Back at the bridge another attack was mounted and failed. A column of 300 Federals charged down the road next to the creek, but at every step they were blasted by riflemen on the opposite bank and by artillery on the hill still farther back. The column disintegrated after the attackers lost nearly half their men.

Eventually, at about 12:30 P.M., a third attack was organized. From a position upstream, Union artillery raked the opposing bluff with grapeshot. While two Union regiments fired their rifles from the top of the slope facing the bridge, another two regiments, the 51st New York and the 51st Pennsylvania, charged down the hill. The plan was to storm straight across the bridge, but Confederate fire forced the regiments to take cover to either side. Lieutenant George Whitman, brother of the poet, later wrote, "We were then ordered to halt and commence fireing, and the way we showered the lead across that creek was noboddys buisness." Soon Confederates were seen leaving their positions and retreating up the hill. As the enemy fire slackened, the two Union regiments followed their color bearers across the bridge in a solid column and fanned out to either side.

It was 1 P.M. by the time the bridge was taken, and another two hours passed while Burnside and Cox brought men and artillery across the creek and organized the troops on the western side. During the interval, General Rodman led 3,200 Yankees across the river at Snavely's Ford, then continued north up a ravine to join the Federals who had crossed the bridge.

At 3 P.M. the Union attack south of Sharpsburg was renewed as more than 8,000 Federals advanced uphill toward the town on a front three-quarters of a mile wide. For the next hour they moved forward by stages, pressing toward Cemetery Hill and reaching the southern edge of Sharpsburg itself. One Virginian described the approach of the Federal line:

> The first thing we saw appear was the gilt eagle that surmounted the pole, then the top of the flag, next the flutter of the stars and stripes itself, slowly mounting, up it rose, then their hats came in sight, still rising the faces emerged, next a range of curious eyes appeared, then such a hurrah as only the Yankee troops could give, broke the stillness, and they surged against us.

Each side fired volley after volley at pointblank range. The Yankees rushed forward, and the lines collided in hand-to-hand combat. Finally the Confederates ran for the rear. "I was afraid of being struck in the *back*," a Southern private recalled, "and I frequently turned half around in running, so as to avoid if possible so disgraceful a wound." As he ran he heard the Yankees cheering in unison, "as if they had gained a game of baseball."

Again, Lee's army seemed to be on the brink of disaster. But then the troops at the left end of the Federal line broke in confusion, suddenly attacked by Confederates who had come up from the south and swung off the road into a line of battle. Major General A.P. Hill's division had marched seventeen miles from Harpers Ferry in eight hours, and now his troops entered the battle without pausing. The shock recoiled down the Federal line, and after Hill got his artillery into action, the Yankees were forced into a general withdrawal toward the bridge.

The Confederates were not strong enough to pursue the Federals, but they regained sole possession of the slopes immediately south of Sharpsburg. To the north their lines were also intact, reformed a few hundred yards to the rear of their original positions. With the approach of dark the fighting died down, and each side began the task of searching the fields for their wounded. Describing the battlefield, a Southern officer wrote:

> The dead and dying lay as thick . . . as harvest sheaves. The pitiable cries for water with appeals for help were much more horrible to listen to than the deadliest sounds of battle. Silent were the dead, and motionless. But here and there were raised stiffened arms; heads made a last effort to lift themselves from the ground; prayers were mingled with oaths, and oaths with delirium, men were wriggling over the earth; and midnight hid all distinction between the blue and the gray.

The Union and Confederate forces prepared for a resumption of the battle at dawn on the 18th. Even after subtracting its losses, the Army of the Potomac was still powerful, numbering more than 62,000 soldiers, a third of them veterans who had not fought on the 17th. But McClellan continued to be apprehensive about a counterattack, and so he did not renew the fighting. Indicating that he would risk nothing, McClellan reported, "I concluded that the success of an attack was not certain. . . . I should have had a narrow view of the condition of the country had I been willing to hazard another battle with less than an absolute assurance of success."

For his part, Lee had only 28,300 exhausted infantry and 4,500 cavalry; nonetheless, for a period he *did* contemplate a sweep to the north, but the odds were too great. So as the day passed and McClellan's inaction showed that the Confederates could retreat in safety, Lee decided to withdraw that night. McClellan made no attempt to interfere, and the entire Army of Northern Virginia, with its artillery, wagon trains of supplies, ambulances and walking wounded, moved out from Sharpsburg in the dark and forded the Potomac at Shepherdstown.

The battle of Antietam is commonly termed a military stalemate by which both sides suffered grievously. Union losses were 2,108 dead, 9,540 wounded (many, of course, maimed for life, or at least invalided out of the war), and 753 missing and for the most part probably dead. The total of 12,401 Yankee casualties was 25 percent of those who went into action. The Confederacy lost about 1,500 dead, 7,750 wounded, and 1,000 missing. Although Confederate losses were marginally less than those of the Union, on a percentage basis they were greater. Moreover, Southern losses were more difficult to replace than those of the populous North.

The battle worked to the disadvantage of the Confederacy in other ways also. Although Lee extricated his battered army from a position where a Union commander more aggressive than McClellan would have crushed the Confederates before they could escape across the Potomac, the fact remained that Lee's invasion was turned back. The British government decided that the moment to recognize the Confederacy had not arrived after all. The failure of the invasion also provided Lincoln with an opportunity to issue the Emancipation Proclamation on September 22, declaring that the war was being fought to end slavery in the rebellious states as well as to restore the Union. Lincoln had been considering this step for two months but had decided to postpone his announcement until the military news was better than it had been all summer. Although the proclamation did not, of course, have any immediate effect on slaves in Confederate territory, and in any case would not take effect until January 1, 1863, it nonetheless reduced further the possibility that the British government, which had outlawed the slave trade and slavery in its own colonies during the first half of the century, would support the South.

Following the battle, Lee withdrew through the Shenandoah Valley, while McClellan remained at Sharpsburg for more than a month. On October 9 Lincoln unexpectedly arrived at McClellan's camp to view the battlefield, review the troops, and confer with the general. "I incline to think that the real purpose of his visit is to

push me into a premature advance into Virginia," McClellan wrote to his wife the next day. As the President and the War Department continued to prod him during the following weeks, McClellan told his wife that he was being bombarded with insults, innuendoes, and accusations "from men whom I know to be greatly my inferior socially, intellectually, & morally! There never was a truer epithet applied to a certain individual than that of the 'Gorilla.'" Nor did McClellan like the President's policies. McClellan had been appalled by the Emancipation Proclamation, which he regarded as unconstitutional. As far as he was concerned, the proper and limited objective of the war was simply to quash the rebellion in the South and reunite the country, whereas emancipation was itself a revolution.

As days and weeks passed and the Union army remained in camp, Lincoln became increasingly disgusted with McClellan's reluctance to take to the field. He chided McClellan for what he called his "over-cautiousness" (Lee had used much the same term in analyzing McClellan's abilities) and even told a friend that so far from being an offensive force, the Army of the Potomac was simply McClellan's bodyguard. Waiting until the army had finally moved into Virginia and until after the fall elections, Lincoln dismissed McClellan on November 7 and replaced him with General Burnside. Two years later McClellan ran for the Presidency against Lincoln but lost by a substantial margin.

As for Burnside, in December 1862, he led the Army of the Potomac to defeat at Fredericksburg, where the Union (but not the Confederacy) suffered losses comparable to the battle of Antietam. General Hooker then took over, but again the Federals were defeated at Chancellorsville in May 1863, ushering in Lee's second invasion of the North, which culminated at Gettysburg.

AUTOMOBILE: From Exits 35 or 38 of the Capital Beltway (I-495) northwest of Washington, take I-270 toward Frederick. As you approach Frederick, exit onto I-70 west toward Hagerstown. Within the space of a few miles, pass the exit for Routes 340 and 15, then exit for Route 40 Alternate toward Braddock Heights and Middletown. Follow Route 40 Alternate 11.4 miles west to Boonsboro, and there turn left onto Route 34 toward Sharpsburg. After 6.3 miles, turn right onto Route 65 in Sharpsburg. Follow Route 65 for 0.9 mile to the entrance to the visitor center for Antietam National Battlefield on the right.

After stopping by the visitor center, which features a short movie depicting the battle, take an automobile tour through the park along the route described below. The automobile tour leads past the Burnside Bridge, jumping off spot for the walk.

From the visitor center, drive north 1 mile past the Dunker Church, then turn right onto Mansfield Avenue in the vicinity of what once was the North Woods. At a T-intersection, turn right onto Smoketown Road, along which Major General Joseph Mansfield's Twelfth Corps advanced from the northeast. Pass a road intersecting from the left in the vicinity of the East Woods, then turn right and continue across the Cornfield, where so much of the fighting occurred. Turn left at the main road, go 0.1 mile, then turn right to a monument marking the area at the West Woods where Sedgewick's division of the Union Second Corps was repulsed.

Turn right back onto the main road, then left onto Smoketown Road. Go 0.2 miles, then turn right to pass the cemetery and farmhouse of the Mumma family. Turn left at a T-intersection and follow Richardson Avenue parallel with the Sunken Road (or Bloody Lane), which Major General Israel Richardson's troops finally captured, only to be stopped as they tried to continue their advance across the field to the right.

From the observation tower, continue along the park road. Cross Route 34 and follow Rodman Avenue below Cemetery Hill. Turn left at the next intersection and follow the road all the way to its end, where there is a parking circle above the Burnside Bridge. The walk described at the end of the chapter starts at the bridge and returns to the parking circle.

To complete the automobile tour, follow the road away from the Burnside Bridge. Pass the intersection with Rodman Avenue, then bear left uphill. Turn right, then turn right again at a T-intersection in order to head north into Sharpsburg. In Sharpsburg, turn right onto Route 34 (East Main Street) and follow it 0.4 mile to Antietam National Cemetery on the right.

WALK: Until recently, the Snavely's Ford Trail, which is merely 2 miles long, was the only footpath maintained by the National Park Service at Antietam National Battlefield. Now, owing to budget reductions, even this short trail is no longer maintained, with the result that damage done by floods remains unrepaired. Because parts of the trail can be muddy, the best time of year to go is the dry season — i.e., late summer and early fall, but not immediately after rain.

From the parking circle for the Burnside Bridge, follow the path as it zigzags downhill. At the end of the bridge nearest the parking lot, descend to the Snavely's Ford Trail, which starts at the edge of Antietam Creek. (As a sign notes, there may be hazards due to lack of maintenance, but as of early 1985, the trail was still passable.)

With the creek on the left, follow the trail downstream. Eventually, at Snavely's Ford, where Brigadier General Isaac Rodman's division waded across the stream, follow the path to the right uphill away from the creek. Continue as the trail climbs to a plateau, then turn left at a T-intersection. Follow the path to the McKinley Monument at the Burnside Bridge parking circle.

BIBLIOGRAPHY

The numbers in parentheses at the end of the citations refer to the chapters in this book that are based on the cited material.

Bacon-Foster, Carra. "Early Records in the Development of the Potomac Route to the West." *Records of the Columbia Historical Society of Washington, D.C.,* Vol. 5, 1912. (9)

Bradley, Harriet F. "Statement on the Burling Tract." Press Release, April 27, 1970. (8)

Brush, Grace Somers, Cecilia Lenk, and Joanne Smith. "Vegetation Map of Maryland." Baltimore: The Johns Hopkins University, 1976. (3)

Caton, Bruce. *The Coming Fury.* Garden City, N.Y.: Doubleday & Company, Inc., 1961. (5)

Caton, Bruce. *Terrible Swift Sword.* Garden City, N.Y.: Doubleday & Company, Inc., 1963. (6, 17, 18)

Clarke, Ella E., editor. "Life on the C. & O. Canal: 1859." *Maryland Historical Magazine,* June, 1960. (13)

Cleaves, Emery T., Jonathan Edwards, Jr., and John D. Glaser. "Geologic Map of Maryland." Baltimore: Maryland Geological Survey, 1968. (3, 10, 11, 16)

Farquhar, Roger Brook. *Old Homes and History of Montgomery County, Maryland.* Silver Spring: Judd & Betweiler, Inc., printers, 1952. (14)

Fitzpatrick, John C., editor. *The Writings of George Washington,* Vol. 36. U.S. Government Printing Office, 1941. (1)

"Fort Washington, Maryland." U.S. Government Printing Office, 1949. (1)

Froelich, Albert J. "Thickness of Overburden Map of Montgomery County, Maryland," Map I-920-B, Miscellaneous Investigations Series. Reston, Va.: U.S. Geological Survey, 1975. (10)

Hack, John T. "Geology of the Brandywine Area and Origin of the Upland of Southern Maryland," Geological Survey Professional Paper 267-A. U.S. Government Printing Office, 1955. (3)

Hahn, Thomas F. *George Washington's Canal at Great Falls, Virginia.* Shepherdstown, W.V.: American Canal and Transportation Center, 1976. (9)

Hedges, James. "Geography, Geology, and Geomorphology of Sugarloaf Mountain, Maryland." Manuscript report for Stronghold, Inc., 1973. (16)

Heine, Cornelius W. "The Chesapeake and Ohio Canal: Testimony to an Age Yet to Come." *Records of the Columbia Historical Society of Washington D.C., 1966-68.* (13)

Hinds, James R. and Edmund Fitzgerald. *Bulwark and Bastion.* Las Vegas: privately printed, 1981. (1)

Hopkins, G.M. *Atlas of Fifteen Miles Around Washington, Including the County of Montgomery, Maryland.* Rockville, Md.: Montgomery County Historical Society, 1975 (reprint). (14, 15)

Hornig, Roberta. "The Burling Tract Battle: They'd Rather Hike Than Fight, But . . ." *The Star*, 3 November 1969. See also numerous contemporaneous newspaper accounts by reporters Thomas Crosby of *The Star*, Sue Johnson of the *Northern Virginia Sun*, Colman McCarthy and Kenneth Bredemeier of *The Post*, and others. (8)

Joseph, Marianne, "Historical Study of 'Woodlands' Site, Seneca Creek State Park, including the Natural History of the Area." Independent Study Project, 1980. (14)

Lee, Ronald F. "Chesapeake and Ohio Canal." *Records of the Columbia Historical Society of Washington, D.C.,* Vol. 40-41, 1940. (13)

McGrain, John W. *The Molinography of Maryland: A Tabulation of Mills, Furnaces, and Primitive Industries.* Towson, Md.: 1968. Revised and expanded, 1976. Microfilm. (14, 15)

McLennan, Jeanne D. "Miocene Sharks Teeth of Calvert County" (pamphlet). Baltimore: Maryland Geological Survey. 1971. (2)

Miller, Helen Hill. *George Mason of Gunston Hall.* Lorton, Va.: The Board of Regents of Gunston Hall, 1958. (4)

Morgan, James Dudley. "Historic Fort Washington on the Potomac." *Records of the Columbia Historical Society of Washington, D.C.,* Vol. 7, 1904. (1)

Nicolay, John G. "The Outbreak of Rebellion" in *Campaigns of the Civil War.* New York: Thomas Yoseloff. (5)

Reed, John C., Jr. and John C. Reed. *Gold Veins Near Great Falls, Maryland,* U.S. Geological Survey Bulletin 1286. U.S. Government Printing Office, 1969. (12)

Reed, John C., Jr., Robert S. Sigafoos, and George W. Fisher. *The River and the Rocks,* U.S. Geological Survey Bulletin 1471. U.S. Government Printing Office, 1980. (11)

Scharf, Thomas J. *History of Western Maryland.* Baltimore: Regional Publishing Company, 1968 (reprint). (14)

Scotford, David M. "Structure of the Sugarloaf Mountain Area, Maryland, as a Key to Piedmont Stratigraphy." *Bulletin of the Geological Society of America,* Vol. 62, January 1951. (16)

Sears, Stephen W. *Landscape Turned Red.* New Haven: Ticknor & Fields, 1983. (6, 17, 18)

Springer, Ethel M. and Thomas F. Hahn. *Canal Boat Children.* Shepherdstown, W.V.: American Canal and Transportation Center, 1981. (13)

Stackpole, Edward J. "Showdown at Sharpsburg" in *The Battle of Antietam.* Eastern Acorn Press, 1983. (18)

Stose, George W. and Anna J. Stose. "Geology of Carroll and Frederick Counties" in *The Physical Features of Carroll County and Frederick County.* Baltimore: Department of Geology, Mines, and Water Resources, Board of Natural Resources, State of Maryland, 1946. (16)

Thane, Elswyth. *Potomac Squire.* Mount Vernon, Va: Mount Vernon Ladies Association, 1963. (4)

Thomas, Byron K. "Stratigraphy of Sugarloaf Anticlinorium and Adjacent Piedmont Area, Maryland." Baltimore, unpublished doctoral dissertation, Johns Hopkins University, 1952. (16)

Williams, Ames W. "The Washington and Old Dominion Railroad." *Records of the Columbia Historical Society of Washington, D.C., 1966-68.* (7)

Young, Joanne (text) and Taylor Lewis (photographs). *George Mason's Gunston Hall.* Lorton, Va.: The Board of Regents of Gunston Hall, 1980. (4)

ORDER FORM

Rambler Books
1430 Park Avenue
Baltimore, MD 21217

Please send me the following books. I understand that I may return any book for a full refund if I am not satisfied.

—— copies of *Country Walks Near Baltimore*
@ $7.95 each.   ——————

—— copies of *Country Walks Near Boston*
@ $7.95 each.   ——————

—— copies of *Country Walks Near Philadelphia*
@ $7.95 each.   ——————

—— copies of *Country Walks Near Washington*
@ $6.95 each.   ——————

—— copies of *More Country Walks Near Washington* @ $7.95 each.   ——————

Maryland residents: Please add 5% sales tax.   ——————

Shipping: $1 for the first book and 25¢ for
each additional book, or   ——————

I can't wait 2-3 weeks for Book Rate. Please
send the books First Class, for which I am
enclosing $2 for the first book and 50¢ for
each additional book.   ——————

Total payment enclosed.   ——————

Send books to (please print):

Name: _____

Address: _____

_____ Zip: _____

ORDER FORM

Rambler Books
1430 Park Avenue
Baltimore, MD 21217

Please send me the following books. I understand that I may return any book for a full refund if I am not satisfied.

_____ copies of *Country Walks Near Baltimore* @ $7.95 each.   _____

_____ copies of *Country Walks Near Boston* @ $7.95 each.   _____

_____ copies of *Country Walks Near Philadelphia* @ $7.95 each.   _____

_____ copies of *Country Walks Near Washington* @ $6.95 each.   _____

_____ copies of *More Country Walks Near Washington* @ $7.95 each.   _____

Maryland residents: Please add 5% sales tax.   _____

Shipping: $1 for the first book and 25¢ for each additional book, or   _____

I can't wait 2-3 weeks for Book Rate. Please send the books First Class, for which I am enclosing $2 for the first book and 50¢ for each additional book.   _____

Total payment enclosed.   _____

Send books to (please print):

Name: _____

Address: _____

_____ Zip: _____